ROBERT MORRIS, AUDACIOUS PATRIOT

Also by Frederick Wagner

PATRIOT'S CHOICE: *The Story of John Hancock*

SUBMARINE FIGHTER OF THE AMERICAN REVOLUTION:
The Story of David Bushnell

FAMOUS UNDERWATER ADVENTURERS

FAMOUS AMERICAN ACTORS AND ACTRESSES
(*with Barbara Brady*)

ROBERT MORRIS
Audacious Patriot

FREDERICK WAGNER

ILLUSTRATED WITH PRINTS
AND PORTRAITS
FROM THE PERIOD

DODD, MEAD & COMPANY
NEW YORK

Copyright © 1976 by Frederick Wagner
All rights reserved
No part of this book may be reproduced in any form
without permission in writing from the publisher
Printed in the United States of America

Library of Congress Cataloging in Publication Data

Wagner, Frederick, 1928–
  Robert Morris, audacious patriot.

  Bibliography: p.
  Includes index.
  SUMMARY: A biography of the Pennsylvania signer of the Declaration of Independence who served as superintendent of finance for the new United States government from 1789–1795.
  1. Morris, Robert, 1734–1806. [1. Morris, Robert, 1734–1806. 2. Statesmen] I. Title.
E302.6.M8W33   973.3′092′4   [B]   [92]   75-38731
ISBN 0-396-07281-X

For my son, Alex

Acknowledgments

This biography, like my earlier books, could not have been written without the limitless patience and help of many librarians in New York City, Philadelphia, Durham, and Clinton. I owe special thanks to the staff of the Central Building of The New York Public Library, as well as to R. N. Williams 2d and Osea McDonald of The Historical Society of Pennsylvania, who, years ago, helped in my search for illustrations for this volume. Of the works listed in the bibliography, I am especially indebted to those by E. James Ferguson, Ellis Paxson Oberholtzer, William Graham Sumner, and Clarence L. Ver Steeg. And to my editor, Joe Ann Daly, my gratitude is considerable. I also must thank my colleagues in the Department of English at Hamilton College and the students in my courses, all of whom help to create a community in which every inhabitant can have a Walden.

Frederick Wagner

Contents

I.	From the Old World to New Fortunes	1
II.	Taxes, Tea Parties, and a Merchant's Marriage	17
III.	A Reluctant Rebel—and a Victory Dearly Bought	26
IV.	The Fall of a City and of a "Worthless Wretch"	39
V.	Hard Cash and a Hard-fought Campaign	52
VI.	After Yorktown: Bank Notes and Morris Notes	83
VII.	Efforts to "Keep the Money-Machine a Going"	97
VIII.	Another Ship to China . . . and the Constitutional Convention	107
IX.	Senator Morris . . . and Speculator Morris	115
X.	From "Castle Defiance" to the Prune Street Jail	128
	Bibliography	135
	Index	141

Illustrations

Following page 58

Robert Morris, Sr.
Mary White Morris
Robert Morris. Portrait by Peale.
The London Coffee House
Morris's home at 190 High Street
The British barracks in Philadelphia
Independence Hall
Signing of the Declaration of Independence
The Announcement of the Declaration of Independence
Robert Morris. From the portrait by Chappel.
"Lemon Hill," the home of Robert Morris
Mount Vernon
Gouverneur Morris, 1780
Robert Morris. Oil miniature by Trumbull, 1790.
Gouverneur Morris. From the painting by Chappel.
Benjamin Franklin
Alexander Hamilton
John Jay
John Paul Jones
Robert Morris. Portrait by Otis and Sully.

The Walnut Street prison
Morris's unfinished home on Chestnut Street
Morris's mansion at Sixth and Market streets and his home at 190 Market Street occupied by Washington

I

From the Old World to New Fortunes

The thirteen-year-old boy who made ready to sail from England for America sometime in 1747 was vividly aware of the perils of sea voyages in the eighteenth century. Raised by his grandmother after his mother's death, Robert Morris had spent his childhood in Liverpool, the bustling port in the west of England where he had been born on January 31, 1734, The boy's father, Robert Morris, Sr., had crossed the Atlantic from England to arrive in Oxford, Maryland, about 1738 as agent for the Liverpool firm of Foster Cunliffe and Sons. When the father sent for his son to join him, he surely advised the boy of the hazards he would encounter on the trip.

Liverpool, which young Morris was to leave behind him forever, had been described by Daniel Defoe, author of *Robinson Crusoe*, as "one of the wonders of Britain." "The town," Defoe noted in *A Tour Through the Whole Island of Great Britain*, "has now an opulent, flourishing, and encreasing trade, not rivalling Bristol in the trade to Virginia and the English island colonies in America only, but in a fair way to exceed and eclipse it, by encreasing every way in wealth and shipping. They trade round the whole island. . . ." In addition, Defoe said, the Liverpool merchants sent ships to Norway, Hamburg, the Baltic, and

Holland, with the result that, "in a word, they are almost become like the Londoners, universal merchants." Defoe also had high praise for "the fineness of the streets, and beauty of the buildings . . . as handsomely built as London itself."

Bob Morris's earliest memories, then, were of trade and merchants and ships and sailing men. Not surprisingly, his interest would be strong in risky and far-ranging trading maneuvers.

We can imagine his emotions as his baggage was stowed in a cabin on one of the Foster Cunliffe vessels. He must have felt the insecurity of being torn away from family, friends, and familiar places to face incalculable dangers, cooped up in what must have seemed a fragile vessel, crowded in with older and more toughened companions, yet all of them apprehensive about the voyage ahead, however well they might mask their fears.

In the eighteenth century crossing the Atlantic often took as long as three months, a crossing beset by gales and sudden and violent squalls, by storms that might blow as long as thirty-six hours. Sometimes the ocean was so rough and stormy that a fire for cooking could not be kept going aboard ship. Wave after wave crashing on the decks would leave the sailors standing in water almost up to their knees. Waves washing through the portholes of the cabins would drench the passengers. Rats seemed to be everywhere; they often spoiled the flour and other provisions. Scurvy broke out; using lime juice as a remedy had not yet been discovered. As week after week passed, fresh water became more and more scarce, and the stench from man and animal grew almost intolerable. But, perhaps worst of all, ship, crew, and passengers were in constant danger from privateers manned by the French or Spanish.

The passengers had little entertainment. After a few weeks of constant companionship the conversation of even the wittiest of men becomes boring. Tempers were frayed—and broke. Occasionally, terrifying excitement welled up when another sail was sighted and none could tell at first whether it was friend or foe. A moment or two of fun might be had from watching "grampuses, turtles, bonetas, porpoises, flying and other fish, common in the Atlantic." Ship and all aboard her were at the mercy of wind and current. At best the voyage was tedious and disagreeable. Bob Morris certainly experienced great relief as the vessel sailed through the capes into Chesapeake Bay.

His father, watching the vessel draw into the wharf at Oxford, Maryland, must have felt considerable pride in the boy he saw on deck. Although Mr. Morris had not seen Bob since his son was four, he had little difficulty recognizing the lad, for the family resemblance was marked. At thirteen Bob had not yet reached his full height of six feet, but he was already tall and husky, and his merry blue eyes and cheerful smile indicated that, in his case at least, sandy hair did not mean a hot temper.

Oxford at this time, according to a contemporary, was "the most commercial port in Maryland, & where the store-keepers, & other retailers, both on the western & eastern side of Chesapeake, repaired to lay in their supplies. . . . Seven or eight large ships, at one time, hath frequently been seen laying at Oxford, completing their lading."

The boy must have felt some constraint amidst the joy of the reunion, for he had not seen his father in more than half his young lifetime. And Robert Morris, Sr., was imposing, a man of importance in Oxford, and a man of importance for his employer, for he was responsible for purchasing and shipping baled tobacco leaf to England. "As a mercantile genius," a friend wrote, " 'twas thought he had not his equal in this land. . . . If he had any public political point to carry, he defeated all opposition. He gave birth to the inspection law on tobacco—& carried it—though opposed by a powerful party." The friend also asserted that Morris, Sr., "was the first who introduced the mode of keeping accounts in money, instead of so many pounds of tobacco—so many yard— so many gallon—so many pound, &c.,—as was formerly the case." This flair of the father's for politics and finances would also distinguish the son when he grew to manhood.

Other traits of the father would be reflected in the son. The older Morris was noted as a jovial companion, a good talker, and a steady friend; in these qualities Bob Morris would resemble his father. Robert Morris, Sr.'s greatest foibles, according to Captain Jeremiah Banning, who knew him, were "a haughty & overbearing carriage, perhaps a too vindictive spirit, & to this may be added an extreme severity to his servants." Bob Morris's enemies would later accuse him of haughtiness and conceit, but even those who hated him most could not charge him with vindictiveness.

Although the senior Morris had amassed a respectable library, his son seems to have inherited little of his father's interest in books—other than those required to keep the accounts of the multitude of enterprises in which as a man he would be ceaselessly involved.

Surprisingly, Bob Morris stayed only briefly with his father in Oxford. Some said that the boy did not get along well with Mrs. Sarah Wise, his father's close friend, and the older Morris's "vindictive spirit" and "extreme severity" may have conflicted with the young boy's independent spirit and exuberance. But perhaps both father and son thought that a better chance for worldly advancement lay elsewhere than in Oxford, Maryland.

As a result, in 1748 Robert Morris, Jr., journeyed from Oxford to Philadelphia, where he was to live in the home of Robert Greenway, a merchant who was a friend of the senior Morris.

The Philadelphia to which foutreen-year-old Robert Morris came in 1748 was a growing port with a population of more than 13,000, claimed as being second only to that of Boston. A young Swedish scientist who visited the town that year noted that "its fine appearance, good regulations, agreeable location, natural advantages, trade, riches, and power are by no means inferior to those of any, even of the most ancient towns in Europe." Moreover, the Swede said, "it has not been necessary to force people to come and settle here; on the contrary, foreigners of different languages have left their country, houses, property, and relations, and have ventured over wide and stormy seas in order to come hither. . . . It has received hosts of people which other countries, to their infinite loss, have either neglected, belittled, or expelled."

As Robert Morris first rode through Philadelphia he could see how it reflected the prosperity the Swedish traveler had noted. The town, which stretched about two miles along the Delaware River and back into the country for almost three-quarters of a mile, was beautifully laid out. All the streets, except for the two nearest the Delaware River, ran in straight lines, making right angles at the intersections. Along many of the streets were pavements of flagstones in front of the houses; the pavements were separated from the streets by series of four-foot posts, which helped protect pedestrians from being trampled underfoot by careless riders on horseback or reckless teamsters driving wagons.

The citizens of Philadelphia offered another protection to pedestrians. The roofs of many houses had gutters, carefully connected to drainpipes. "By this means," noted a visitor, "those who walk under them when it rains or when the snow melts need not fear being wet by the water from the roofs." Bob noticed that many of the houses were built of bricks, some of limestone, with the roofs usually made of cedar shingles, although some of the newer houses had roofs of slate tiles.

Soon after arriving in Philadelphia, Morris grew aware that Wednesday and Saturday were the two market days, except in summer, when almost every day was market day because provisions would not keep for long in the Philadelphia heat. The principal market, near the courthouse, began about five o'clock in the morning and ended about nine o'clock in the morning. On market days the country people from Pennsylvania and New Jersey would bring to town seasonal crops and other farm products.

Although Greenway arranged for young Bob to be tutored, the boy detested schoolwork, and soon he was apprenticed to the merchant Charles Willing. The Willing store was in Dock Creek Harbor at Hamilton's Wharf, "the second one above the entrance." Willing's eldest son, Thomas, educated in England, was not quite three years older than Robert Morris, and the two would become close friends for most of their lives.

The ruddy-cheeked, blue-eyed apprentice who trudged along

the bustling Philadelphia waterfront one summer morning in 1750 was filled with a sense of optimism and well-being. At sixteen, Morris felt himself to be in an enviable position. He had been in Philadelphia less than three years, yet already he was on the way to success.

The young man never ceased being excited by the great variety of merchandise handled by the Willing firm. It sold, as its advertisements proclaimed, "European and East India goods, suitable for the season. Also West India rum, muscovado sugar, bohea and hyson teas, Bristol beer, Herefordshire cyder, Gloucester cheese, anvils, hammers, sledges and vises, Vidonia and Sherry wines, long and short pipes, cordage and anchors, window glass . . . , and Welsh and West country servants." These were but some of its commodities, for it also sold broadcloth and gloves, and such staples as salt and flour.

Philadelphia was constantly increasing as a commercial center; the never-ending hustle and clamor along the wharves testified to that. Local merchants were engaged in a flourishing trade. Day after day Morris watched ships sail from the wharves, ships bound for England and Ireland, for Madeira and Lisbon, for the West Indies, New England, and the Southern colonies. And day after day he came into contact with the thriving farmers from the fertile lands stretching from Philadelphia west into Pennsylvania, south into the Potomac Valley, and north into New Jersey.

On one of these summer days a letter reached Robert Greenway from an Oxford friend of the elder Morris. The letter contained news that astounded Greenway and was a tremendous shock to his young ward. Robert Morris, Sr., only thirty-nine years old, was dead.

The story of how he met his death was related later by his granddaughter. A merchant ship with a cargo from Foster Cunliffe had arrived at Oxford. Mr. Morris, Sr., made plans to entertain a group of friends at dinner aboard ship, but the night before the dinner he dreamed that he would be mortally wounded as he returned from the ship to the wharf by a freak misfiring of the ship's guns. The dream was so terrifyingly vivid that Morris decided he would not attend his own party. When he attempted to make excuses to the captain, the captain promised that the ship's guns would not fire the customary salute honoring a guest leaving the ship. The party was festive; even the apprehensive host forgot his fears. As the happy group was about to leave, the captain reported that the members of the crew were very unhappy because they would not receive the customary glass of grog as a reward for firing the salute. Morris gave way, but insisted that the salute should not be fired until he gave the signal by waving his handkerchief. As the small boat carrying Morris and the other dinner guests got about halfway to shore, one of the ladies gaily waved her handkerchief in farewell. Taking this gesture as the signal, the crew fired the salute. The wadding from one of the shots, passing through the backboard of the boat, struck Morris's arm a little above the elbow and broke the bone. With proper surgical treatment, the bone and wound might have healed, but blood poisoning set in, and within a few days Robert Morris, Sr., was dead.

Morris's friend, Mrs. Sarah Wise, was bequeathed £250, two silver tankards and all his clothing; an additional £100 was provided for the child to whom she was about to give birth. This child, who would be named Thomas Morris, was Robert Morris, Jr.'s half brother; he was to cause trouble for everyone who knew him. The bulk of the estate, about £2;000, was left to the legitimate son, sixteen-year-old Robert. The home of Robert Morris, Sr., in Oxford still exists; it now houses the gracious Robert Morris Inn.

Although Bob had seen little of his father, the death must have struck the boy with considerable impact, for he was now alone in the New World. At this time even his employer, Charles Willing, a kind and fatherly man, was absent in England on business. Young Morris had no one on whom to rely but himself, yet self-reliance was a quality he would always have in abundance.

A story circulated that, while Charles Willing still was abroad,

Bob Morris successfully executed the first of many dazzling financial maneuvers. A friend, on board a ship from England that had just reached the mouth of the Delaware, dispatched a messenger to Morris with the news that the price of flour had risen suddenly and sharply. Young Robert Morris immediately rushed out and, on behalf of the Willing firm, contracted for all the flour that could be found in and around Philadelphia. The older merchants, thinking him a remarkably foolish young man, laughed and sold—only to discover a day later that they were the butt of the joke.

When Charles Willing returned from England, he was proud of Morris, and he was especially proud of the way his son Thomas had managed the firm's affairs in his absence; by November, 1751, the firm was advertising itself as "Charles Willing and Son." During the early 1750's Robert Morris was given increasing responsibilities with the firm, although the letters he wrote were usually signed, "For my Masters, C. W. & Son, R. M."

The years between sixteen and twenty-one were increasingly busy ones for Robert Morris. He worked eagerly at any task that came his way, but he was happiest when allowed opportunities to speculate, opportunities in which the chances of disaster were about even with the chances of spectacular success. Even in his teens Morris passionately loved running risks, taking chances, daring to juggle transactions as if he had three hands.

These years, 1750 to 1755, were eventful for the town of Philadelphia. In November, 1754, the birthday of King George II was celebrated in Philadelphia by a ball at the State House, given by the governor of Pennsylvania. About a hundred ladies attended; slightly more men were present so that no lady would be left unattended at any point. Couples danced in the Assembly Chamber, and the scraping of fiddles could be heard throughout the building and on the street outside. Although young Morris, still an apprentice, would not have received an invitation, he could scarcely have resisted wandering along the street to listen to the fiddles and to see what he could glimpse through the large windows. Within a few years he would be a central figure at such festivities.

Hostilities with the French already had begun to trouble the colonies. In the summer of 1754, out in the Ohio Valley young George Washington, barely two years Morris's senior, had been forced to yield Fort Necessity to a large French force under Coulon de Villiers. News of the outbreak of hostilities actually was good news for the firm of Charles Willing and Son, for war always brought an upsurge in trade.

Soon after the Birthday Ball, in the midst of the excitement and arguments, the recruiting and mustering growing out of the French and Indian War, as the struggle would be called, a fear approaching panic gripped Philadelphia. A pestilence was spreading through the town, a sort of ship-fever or typhus that had sprung from the unhealthy conditions on the crowded vessels bringing the Palatines, German immigrants, to Pennsylvania.

One of the most eminent of the Philadelphians struck down by the epidemic was merchant Charles Willing. On November 29, 1754, Robert Morris wrote to one of the firm's correspondents, "I believe by the time I have finished this, Mr. C. W. will be no more. He now lies in the agonies of death, occasioned by a nervous fever which seized him about a week ago. His son and whole family are almost distracted and incapable of any kind of business...." Morris's fears proved to be well-founded; Charles Willing died the following day at the age of forty-five. Robert Morris had, in effect, lost a second father.

But at twenty Morris was too resilient to let grief make him morbid. Willing's death brought him increased responsibilities, and life in eighteenth-century Philadelphia abounded in excitement. Early in 1755 Morris observed with fascination several groups of Indians who visited the town. First came a band of Cherokees, who had escaped from Canada, where they had been carried as prisoners by the French, and were now journeying homeward. Before the Cherokees departed, a deputation of Mohawks arrived for a series of conferences with the authorities of the Province of Pennsylvania.

In June, General Edward Braddock started his march from Fort Cumberland to confront the French at Fort Duquesne; the governor of Pennsylvania appointed the nineteenth as a day of fasting and prayer for the success of the expedition. But fasting and prayers were not enough; Braddock's forces suffered a ruinous defeat at the Battle of the Wilderness on July 9. Braddock himself received a mortal wound, and Lieutenant Colonel Washington led the pitiful remnant of the once-glorious force of British regulars and colonials back to Fort Cumberland.

In the latter part of August troops arrived in Philadelphia and set up camp. An almost uncontrollable panic over Braddock's defeat had seized the city. Riots seemed imminent. Philadelphians feared an attack by the French and Indians at any moment. And they feared almost as much a torrent of refugees from the western parts of Pennsylvania, where the war was being waged in earnest. Although the Pennsylvania Assembly did practically nothing to provide for the troops, the everyday citizens opened their hearts and homes. The women of Market Street and Church Alley formed an association to provide the soldiers with apple pies and rice puddings.

Apple pies, rice puddings, and general good will eased the tensions that had been threatening. On Monday, September 22, 1755, the gentlemen of the army gave a ball at the State House for "the Ladies and Gentlemen of the City," the hosts being some of the surviving officers of General Braddock's battered forces. One reason for giving the ball was to celebrate Sir William Johnson's victory on September 8 over Baron Dieskau and the French and Indian forces at Lake George. The previous week troops and citizens participated in public demonstrations over the victory, marked by bonfires and "many curious Fire-works plaid off." Another reason for the ball was to express the soldiers' gratitude for the kindness shown them by the citizens of Philadelphia.

Further effects of the French and Indian War were witnessed by the Philadelphians that fall, when more than 450 Acadians arrived at the port and were distributed among several counties. The Acadians were French colonists who had tilled their farms in Nova Scotia under more than forty years of British rule. But with renewed conflict, the British feared that the Acadians would incite the Indians to go on the warpath, and so the British authorities decided to lay waste the Acadians' homesteads and to scatter them throughout the American colonies. On their arrival in the various ports along the coast, their plight seemed as wretched and heartbreaking as that of any displaced persons in the course of history.

In the late fall horrifying reports reverberated through the streets of Philadelphia that a large body of Indians had fallen upon several counties in the Province, murdering, burning, and laying waste. By mid-December the savages had approached to within sixty-five miles of Philadelphia.

In the meantime, Robert Morris had zealously and shrewdly continued his duties in the offices of the Willing warehouse, now located on a wharf near Front and Walnut streets. In February, 1756, having finished his seven-year apprenticeship, he had the opportunity to fulfill a long-cherished desire to visit the "Sugar Islands." His friend and employer, Thomas Willing, sent him to Jamaica aboard the *Severn*, in charge of disposing of a cargo of provisions. Morris's letter of introduction from Willing said in part, ". . . as he is an entire stranger to Jamaica, I beg leave to introduce him to your acquaintance, being confident you will find him an honest worthy young fellow." If Morris had wished, he could have taken on another cargo and sailed with it to Lisbon and London. But, having much less taste for physical adventure than for financial derring-do, he sold ship as well as cargo in Jamaica and returned to Philadelphia. The round trip had held more than enough peril to satisfy him. On this occasion, as on others, he showed no desire to return to his native land. To him America was the land of promises fulfilled, and his heart and mind looked forward to her future, which, even when he was twenty-two, he regarded as inextricably linked with his own future.

In October, Morris was on the way to Jamaica again, aboard a new brigantine also named the *Severn*, of which he was one-fourth owner, the other three shares belonging to Thomas Willing. Once in Kingston, Morris had many conversations with a Mr. Sharp about the two joining in a partnership. Sharp wrote to Willing for advice, who answered that he regarded Morris very highly and would be delighted to have him "advantageously engaged anywhere." Sharp wrote again. This time Willing replied that he was reluctant to interfere. Bob Morris was entirely his own master and ought to be able to decide "what's most for his own interest and advantage." Morris decided that his advantage was best served by remaining with Willing.

In February, 1757, the seafaring Morris was thrust into a hair-raising adventure. Near Cuba the *Severn* was attacked and chased by two French privateers. The crew, beaching the brig on the shores of Cuba at low tide, escaped inland, but when the tide came in and set the vessel afloat, it was captured. A story—apparently without basis in fact—circulated that Morris, captured by the French and cruelly treated, was finally put ashore without a farthing. Then as always, so the story went, his ingenuity asserted itself. He repaired a Frenchman's watch, and the grateful Frenchman paid his transportation to a port, where he found a ship homeward bound. In fact, Morris was unable to make his way back to Philadelphia until early April, when he was heartened to be reassured that insurance had covered most of the cost of the captured brigantine. He began to see himself as a man whom the wheel of fortune would always bring back up to the top.

And later in April his good fortune seemed almost boundless, for he was taken into partnership with Thomas Willing. Not quite a decade of hard, daring, quick-witted work had brought him, at twenty-three, to the head of one of the most important firms of merchants in America. Thomas Willing wrote to his cousin in England that the partnership would enable him and Morris to transact business "to more advantage than either could do singly."

The years immediately following were hectic ones. Even after the surrender of Canada to the British by the French in 1760, the war dragged on until the Treaty of Paris was signed in 1763. The war meant that profits and perils both ran high. Morris and other merchants would gather daily in the London Coffee House, not far from the Willing and Morris warehouse, a meeting place that functioned as a combination brokerage house, bank, chamber of commerce, and bulletin board where news was posted from a multitude of sources—from captains of ships newly arrived in port, from correspondents abroad, from foreign newspapers. The London Coffee House was a noisy place, noisy with the hubbub of voices within and noisy from the almost unbroken procession on the street outside of wagons bringing farm products to the wharves. Teamsters shouted, whips cracked, and wagon wheels rattled over the cobblestones. A contemporary noted that, "At this Coffee House, so begun, the Governor and other persons of note ordinarily went at set hours to sip their coffee from the hissing urn, and some . . . had their known stalls."

Robert Morris and nearly every other citizen of Philadelphia, now, with a population of more than 23,000, larger than either Boston or New York, found the city almost unbearable during the summer heat. Awnings were hung over shop windows and doors to keep off the glare of the sun. Some of the houses had balconies where one could sit in the evening, and practically every house had a bench on either side of the front door where the householders might hope to catch a breath of cool air. Morris was determined to achieve a home outside the city as soon as he could afford one—and could afford a wife to share it with him.

Astute as Willing and Morris were, they were fallible. Records show that a certain John White appeared in Philadelphia in 1760 with a manner and credentials so mesmerizing that he obtained nearly £4,000 credit from almost two dozen individuals and mercantile houses, among them the firm of Willing and Morris. With the money White built a ship, loaded her with cargo, and then announced that, having sent the vessel to sea, he would continue to use Philadelphia as the base of his operations. Thereupon, Mr. White and his wife took a coach to New Castle, where the vessel was waiting, and White, wife, vessel, cargo, and the £4,000 disappeared forever, at least so far as the credulous creditors in Philadelphia were concerned.

The Reverend Andrew Burnaby, an English visitor who arrived in Philadelphia in mid-June, 1760, was tremendously impressed by the city, but he noted what he considered a dangerous tendency:

They are great republicans, and have fallen into the same errors in their ideas of independency as most of the other colonies have. They are by far the most enterprizing people upon the continent. As they consist of several nations, and talk several languages, they are aliens in some respect to Great Britain; nor can it be expected that they should have the same filial attachment to her which her own immediate offspring have. However, they are quiet, and concern themselves but little, except about getting money.

Burnaby here failed to remark on the large Quaker population in the Quaker City, a group that was highly conservative and would resist "ideas of independency." And many non-Quaker citizens of Philadelphia, Morris and Willing among them, in 1760 viewed the republicans with suspicion.

At twenty-six, Robert Morris was one of those especially concerned about getting money. Ambitious though he was, the good-looking bachelor had ample energies for activities other than work. He was sociable, and he had his eye on society. His love of good food was evident: his figure gradually was changing from stocky to stout, but it had not yet reached the proportions that would prompt Alexander Hamilton's sister-in-law to write to her sister, "Don't let Alexander get fat, or he will be [as] unable to flirt as Robert Morris." Morris already had established a reputation for being bold, sensible, and agreeable. He was also proud and passionate, and he had a flair for making violent enemies as well as affectionate friends.

A young bachelor about town could entertain himself with a variety of pleasures. Frequent balls and banquets were given at the State House, to which Morris, now that he had proved his ability to make money, would often be invited, unless the event had to do with politics, in which Morris so far had not been active. The young women of Philadelphia society, a foreign visitor reported, were "exceedingly handsome and polite" and "would not make bad figures even in the first assemblies of Europe." In the summer, to escape the heat of the city, young couples would form groups to journey out into the country toward Germantown or to ramble along the banks of the Schuylkill River and stop at a pleasant spot for tea or dinner. The Schuylkill itself, with the rocks and groves along its banks, was romantic and picturesque. Boats and fishing tackle were available. The couples, a contemporary reported, could thus "divert themselves with walking, fishing, going upon the water, dancing, singing, conversing, or just as they please." In the winter, in addition to many balls and dances, young men and young women would bundle themselves up warmly against the weather and set out on sleighing parties.

Despite his social activities, in the early 1760's Robert Morris assumed more and more of the burden of running the firm, for Thomas Willing had become increasingly involved in politics and in love. Within six months in 1763, Willing was elected mayor of Philadelphia and was married to the charming eighteen-year-old Ann McCall; Willing was fourteen years her senior.

George II had died, and George III had become King. William Penn's grandson, John, had been elected governor of the Province of Pennsylvania; and the Treaty of Paris had been signed. During all this period the trade of Great Britain with the American colonies, and especially with the port of Philadelphia, had been increasing at a rapid rate. On one September day in 1763 an observer counted 134 vessels anchored at the wharves along the Delaware River. "So that should Philadelphia merchants have occasion to block trade, the mere possibility would be a powerful club to be feared by European houses, as Parliament and the Crown were soon to see." Among the most powerful of the Philadelphia merchants was Robert Morris.

II

Taxes, Tea Parties, and a Merchant's Marriage

At high water on Saturday, October 5, 1765, the *Royal Charlotte*, a ship from London under the protection of a man-of-war, came up the Delaware River and anchored before the city of Philadelphia. Its arrival was greeted by an uproar that would echo and re-echo throughout the streets for decades to come. All the ships at anchor flew their flags at half-mast; drums muffled in crepe were beaten through the streets; and the bells of Christ Church and the State House tolled mournfully for hours. By four o'clock a large, angry crowd with the temper of a mob had gathered in the yard of the State House for a general town meeting.

The reason for the uproar was that the most important item in the cargo of the *Royal Charlotte* was the detested "Stamps," which had aroused the subjects of King George III to a frenzy. In March, 1765, Parliament, to raise revenue for the support of the military establishment in America, had passed the first direct tax it had ever levied upon America. Almost every piece of paper used in any sort of business in the colonies was to be taxed: legal papers, wills, licenses, deeds, mortgages, leases, bills of lading, customs clearances, almanacs, newspapers, books, pamphlets, playing cards. The Stamp Act, scheduled to go into effect November 1, already had provoked riots in Boston. The Philadelphians seemed determined not to lag behind the Bostonians.

The protesters ranged from laborers to the town's most prominent merchants. Among the merchants was Robert Morris, at thirty-one an imposing figure, tall, heavily built, with a florid complexion, recognized by everyone around him as a financial wizard. At the town meeting Morris was one of six appointed to call on John Hughes, a prosperous shopkeeper who had been appointed Stamp Master, and demand his resignation.

When Morris and the other members of the committee arrived, Hughes, claiming to be deathly ill, was in bed, but the committee insisted on confronting him in his chambers. They warned him that the crowd in the State House yard was so angry that it might march on Hughes's home and demolish it. Hughes quibbled; he could not resign, he said, because the document appointing him had not yet arrived. How, he asked, could he resign from a position he did not yet hold? Robert Morris, speaking for the committee, insisted that Hughes must swear that he would do nothing to enforce the Stamp Act in Pennsylvania before it was enforced in other colonies. Hughes reluctantly but prudently agreed; his stone house was well built, but it had not been built to withstand a siege.

Returning to the State House yard, Morris and his fellows found the seething crowd in no mood to accept a compromise; someone suggested they march on Hughes's home at once to force him to resign. But the committee prevailed, and those at the meeting finally agreed to send a written request for Hughes's resignation, a request which said in part, "a great Number of the Citizens of Philadelphia, . . . do demand of Mr. John Hughes, . . . that he will give them Assurance, under his Hand, that he will not execute that Office; and expect that he will give them a candid, fair and direct answer by Monday next, at Ten o'Clock, when he will be waited on for that Purpose."

Although Hughes did not yield without additional maneuvering and delays, on Monday afternoon his resignation was read aloud to the people, who greeted it with applause.

After October 5 unrest and resistance to Britain's policies mounted. On October 25, a week before the Stamp Act was to take effect, about four hundred merchants—with Robert Morris and Thomas Willing prominent among the leaders—assembled and drew up what became known as nonimportation resolutions. The merchants swore to order no new goods from England until the repeal of the Stamp Act. Pennsylvania-owned vessels about to return from England might bring back staples: coal, earthenware, pipes, grindstones, and iron posts. The merchants also declared that, after the start of the new year, they would refuse to sell any goods on commission from British firms.

The day before the Stamp Act became effective newspapers appeared with thick black bands of mourning for the death of Liberty. The skull and crossbones were conspicuously displayed. All day long on November 1 muffled church bells tolled. By mid-November the nonimportation resolutions were published, and in December homespun clothing was being advertised. Philadelphians agreed not to eat lamb or mutton, so that sheep would be raised only for wool for domestic products. The day after Christmas a few pieces of paper bearing the detested stamps were set afire to the cheers of a crowd at the London Coffee House.

The events surrounding the Stamp Act brought Robert Morris increasingly into public affairs. In January, 1766, recognizing his abilities, the Pennsylvania Assembly appointed him to a newly established nine-man board, the Wardens of the Port of Philadelphia, to examine and license pilots and to regulate the piloting of ships up the Delaware River to the port.

Rumors reached Morris in March that the Stamp Act had been repealed, and, on May 19, Captain Wise of the brig *Minerva* arrived at the port with official confirmation. Wise was invited to the London Coffee House, where he joined the crowd of celebrants drinking punch and was showered with presents for his entire crew; the most splendid gift was reserved for him: a gold-laced hat, a symbol of the city's gratitude to the bearer of welcome news.

For Morris and other Philadelphians the next few days were

filled with revelry. The night of May 20 almost every street in the city was brilliantly lit. The ladies, always ingenious, had the lamps hung in different positions with dazzling effect. Huge bonfires blazed, and round them crowds gathered, breaking open kegs of beer to celebrate the victory. The following day Morris was undoubtedly one of the three hundred eminent townspeople invited by the governor and the mayor for a feast in the gallery of the State House. "At the same time," an old account says, "it was unanimously resolved to dress themselves at the approaching birthday of King George III in new suits of English manufacture, and to give their homespun and patriotic garments to the poor." At the conclusion of this elegant dinner, twenty-one toasts were drunk, and after each toast a seven-gun salute was fired by the cannon in the State House yard. That evening church bells rang cheerfully and constantly, more bonfires blazed, and the crowd consumed more strong beer.

In celebrating this victory most Philadelphians also were giving vent to relief that resistance to Britain had ended, that the old peaceful ways of life and business could be resumed. In Boston, however, resistance did not yield so easily. Late in 1767 the Bostonians boycotted consumption of British goods, and in March, 1768, they revived nonimportation. A month later New Yorkers volunteered to join the movement if the merchants of Philadelphia also would join, but the Philadelphians took almost a year before deciding to participate. Here, as with later events, the men of Philadelphia showed themselves to be considerably more conservative than the fiery-tempered men of Boston.

With an equilibrium apparently re-established in politics and in business, Robert Morris found himself thinking more and more about marriage. Now approaching thirty-five, he increasingly felt the desire to pause—at least for a moment or two—in his pursuit of mercantile success in order to pursue a wife. His affability and obvious appreciation when being entertained meant that he rarely lacked invitations to dine out, but dining out night after night ultimately becomes tedious for even the most convivial of men.

Philadelphia was noted for its beautiful young women. Many of those who lacked beauty abounded in wit, and most of those who possessed neither beauty nor wit could justly claim to be rich. Morris's glance finally lighted on a young woman about fifteen years his junior who was described by a contemporary as "elegant, accomplished, and rich." She was "in every respect qualified to carry the felicity of connubial life to its highest perfection." She was celebrated by a local poet as "lovely White," and everyone who knew brown-eyed Mary White agreed with the poet's praise. Her father was Colonel Thomas White, a lawyer and surveyor; her brother William would become the first bishop of the Episcopal church in America. The courtship was swift; the couple was married on March 2, 1769. The following December, just six days before Christmas, their first son, Robert, was born. Two others came soon: Thomas, on February 26, 1771; William, on August 9, 1772.

As soon as Morris was married and settled into a city home on Front Street, facing the Delaware River, he began moving ahead with plans for the summer home he had long promised himself. In 1770 he bought an eighty-acre farm on the eastern bank of the Schuylkill River, where, three years later, he built "The Hills," a two-story square house with a chimney at each corner and piazzas on two sides. The country estate became a passion. Morris imported cattle and sheep to browse on the slopes surrounding "The Hills." Oranges and pineapples were grown in the hothouses; his icehouse is said to have been the first in America built for a private home. The estate also boasted two farmhouses, a separate house for the gardener, another for the cows, still another for the coaches, and, in addition, stables, barns, sheds, cribs. The place was magnificent, but its magnificence satisfied Morris only for a while.

While "The Hills" was being created, Morris found himself involved in an embarrassing squabble between John and Richard

Penn, grandsons of the illustrious William Penn. John, after serving as governor of Pennsylvania, had returned to England in 1771. Richard, succeeding to the governorship, apparently thought he could hold the position as long as he wished; to his chagrin, he learned in 1773 that John was to return and again become governor. Richard sulked publicly, especially after John was inaugurated on August 30, a ceremony from which the outgoing governor was conspicuously absent.

But Richard had made himself so popular with the merchants that they planned a testimonial dinner for him two weeks after the inauguration of his rival. Robert Morris was chosen to preside, a challenge that threatened even his imperturbability, for he knew that John Penn, the person of highest rank at the banquet, must be seated on his right, and that Richard Penn, the guest of honor, must be seated on his left. At the banquet, Morris needed all his considerable aplomb and appetite to make his way through the seemingly endless courses, for neither brother spoke to the other, nor even glanced in the other's direction. Morris must have sighed with relief when the time came for him to rise, lift his glass, and offer a toast, "Gentlemen, I give you the King." A twenty-one gun salute was fired outside in the State House yard. Nineteen more toasts were offered, each followed by a salute from the guns. Fortunately for Morris and the other merchants, the brothers maintained their dignity and even their sobriety throughout the ceremony, and the banquet ended without calamity.

Meanwhile, Morris and the other Philadelphia merchants—and merchants in Boston, New York, and Charleston as well—were on the verge of becoming involved in a skirmish of considerably greater significance.

During the spring of 1773 the British Parliament had passed the Tea Act, a bill designed to rescue the foundering East India Company by enabling it to sell tea in America at prices lower than the colonial merchants could obtain elsewhere; the threat of monopoly and restraint of trade was a dangerous one to the colonials, and they resisted it vehemently.

In Philadelphia, at a town meeting on October 16 at the State House, Morris and his fellow merchants drew up a statement resolving that anyone who in any way abetted the East India Company's attempt to export tea to America was "an Enemy to his Country." A committee called upon those in Philadelphia to whom tea had been consigned; most of the consignees agreed immediately not to accept any tea sent to them, but a few were evasive.

For the next month and a half newspapers and intercolonial correspondence kept public indignation aflame, and on December 1 the *Pennsylvania Gazette* announced: "The Ship Polly, Captain Ayres, from London, for this Port, having the DETESTED TEA on board, sailed from Gravesend on the 27th of September, and may be hourly expected.—*Americans! be wise—be virtuous.*" Consignees were immediately visited again by committees or served with public notices. Pilots were warned not to guide the *Polly* up the Delaware. On Christmas Eve word reached Philadelphia that a mob in Boston had tossed the contents of 342 chests of tea into Boston Harbor. This news of the Boston Tea Party was greeted jubilantly; Philadelphians looked forward to holding a tea party of their own. On Christmas Day a messenger galloped into town to reveal that the *Polly*, "an old black ship," even though she could not hire a pilot, had managed to reach Chester by following another ship up the Delaware.

The next day, a Sunday, a delegation hailed the *Polly* at Gloucester Point. Captain Ayres, "*a short fat Fellow*, and a little *obstinate* withal," reluctantly agreed to accompany the group back to Philadelphia, where, the following morning, he was brought before a town meeting in the State House yard of eight thousand citizens who had gathered in response to the call for "every inhabitant who wishes to preserve the liberty" to turn out "to consider what is best to be done in this alarming crisis." Ayres, obstinate though he was, possessed enough common sense to yield to the mob and agreed not to unload his cargo. The next afternoon a crowd on the wharf cheered him on his way to the *Polly* and to England. But some men in Philadelphia did not cheer the events that had taken place, events which they saw as essentially a mob's lawless act. Yet that act, though less theatrical than the deed done in Boston, was equally effective in removing the East India Company's tea.

The new year brought further dissension. Parliament, to punish Massachusetts for the Boston Tea Party, decreed that after May 31, 1774, ships in Boston Harbor could unload no cargo except military stores and whatever shipments of food and fuel customs officials deemed necessary; the ban would be lifted only when the East India Company was recompensed for its loss. Silversmith Paul Revere, who would soon make his famous midnight ride, galloped into Philadelphia in May with the news. June 1, the day the act took effect, was observed as a day of mourning in Philadelphia. Many of the shops were shut, ships flew colors at half-mast, the bells of Christ Church, muffled, were tolled solemnly from morn till night. "Sorrow, mixed with indignation," noted Philadelphian Christopher Marshall, "seemed pictured in the countenances of the inhabitants, and indeed the whole city wore the aspect of deep distress, being a melancholy occasion."

A week later Governor John Penn was petitioned by nearly nine hundred citizens to call a session of the Pennsylvania Assembly to discuss the actions of the British Parliament toward America. Penn's response was courteous but firm: "Gentlemen, upon occasions when the peace, order, and tranquillity of the Province require it, I shall be ready to convene the Assembly; but as that does not appear to be the case at present, I cannot think such a step would be expedient or consistent with my duty."

Robert Morris, Thomas Willing, and other leading citizens would not be silenced. On Saturday, June 18, as Christopher Marshall recorded, a "very large and respectable meeting of the freeholders and freemen of this city met in the State House yard, where Thomas Willing and John Dickinson were chairmen, when they entered into six spirited resolves, and chose forty-three persons as committeemen to transact their affairs." The meeting agreed that the Boston Port Bill was illegal and that the colonies should be urged to convoke a Continental Congress to consider the best ways to secure their liberties and peace. By September 5 the First Continental Congress, to which eleven colonies sent delegates, was at work—or at odds—in Carpenters' Hall, two blocks from the State House. The Congress appealed to King George III to respect the rights of the American colonists, recommended that exports to and imports from Britain be banned, and adjourned to meet again in May, 1775.

Although neither Morris nor Willing was a delegate to the First Continental Congress, both men were intensely involved with the proceedings. Morris, especially, regarded his private business interests and the public interests of the colonies as inseparably intertwined. A healthy economy meant a healthy country, and increasingly he questioned whether either could remain healthy if vitality were constantly being drained by mercantile interests in far-off London. True, England was the mother country, but the umbilical cord seemed to be working in reverse: the child was nourishing the mother. Yet Morris's attitude at this point was essentially conservative. He was determined to uphold his rights, private and public, but he hoped for reconciliation with Britain, not separation from her. He regarded with suspicion such Boston firebrands as Sam Adams.

Amid the public tumult Morris's marriage proceeded serenely. Mary—or "Molly," as she often was called—now twenty-six, gave birth to their first daughter, Hetty, on July 30, 1774. Travel between his country house, "The Hills," and his offices in the city added extra hours to Morris's hectic schedule, but the love of his family was a dominant force in this energetic man of forty. His responsibilities to his family and to the public were increasing.

III

A Reluctant Rebel—and a Victory Dearly Bought

One afternoon late in April, 1775, Robert Morris and about a hundred other eminent Philadelphians sat down at a banquet at the City Tavern in honor of St. George, the patron saint of England. All were members of the St. George's Society for the Assistance of Englishmen in Distress, an organization which Morris, now its vice-president, had helped found in 1772. On the present occasion Morris, as presiding officer, was leading the toasts to King George III and other members of the royal family when an express rider, having just dismounted from his panting horse in front of the tavern, burst into the hall with news of the battles at Lexington and Concord on April 19. The guests, hastily rushing out, overturned tables and chairs in their pell-mell flight. Morris, legend has it, with his glass raised, found himself facing an almost empty room and, instead of completing the toast, firmly pledged his service to the colonies in the struggle that now appeared inevitable. But a pledge of service did not mean a pledge for independence.

Tempers ran high in the days that followed. Dissenters from the common sentiment were treated roughly; one shoemaker, for example, was dragged to the Coffee House and forced to beg forgiveness "for his illiberally and wickedly villifying the measures of Congress . . . and the people of New England." Militia companies formed, and even some spirited Quakers sought permission to participate in military exercises.

On May 5 the *Pennsylvania Packet* docked from London, bearing an impressive cargo, Dr. Benjamin Franklin, Pennsylvania's most distinguished citizen, returning after many years in England "to the satisfaction of his friends and the lovers of liberty." Soon afterward delegates to the Second Continental Congress began arriving, among them George Washington, Patrick Henry, Richard Henry Lee, Benjamin Harrison, John Hancock, and John and Sam Adams. Those traveling overland were met about six miles outside the city by five hundred members of the militia and conducted into Philadelphia to triumphant music and hearty cheers. On the day that Ethan Allen and Benedict Arnold captured Fort Ticonderoga, the Second Continental Congress began its duties in the State House on Chestnut Street.

Although Robert Morris had not yet been selected as a delegate to Congress, by early July he was serving as vice-president to Franklin's president on the Committee of Safety appointed by the Pennsylvania Assembly to supervise military powers within the province. Morris was quickly made chairman of a subcommittee "to procure any quantity of powder in their power with the utmost expedition." Morris eagerly attacked the multitude of problems involved in planning fortifications for the Delaware River and in organizing the militia and supplying it with arms and ammunition. His zeal and efficiency were recognized and rewarded. In October, 1775, he was elected to the Pennsylvania Assembly, and in November he joined the Second Continental Congress. All the daring shrewdness that had brought him eminence as a private merchant now served him well as a public figure.

Within a few months Morris was a member of the two most important committees appointed by the new Congress, the Secret Committee and the Committee of Secret Correspondence. He succeeded his partner Thomas Willing as chairman of the Secret Committee, authorized to export produce and to import arms and ammunition, as well as such supplies as medicines, blankets, metals, and cotton goods. The Secret Committee (which eventually was renamed the Committee of Commerce and was the forerunner of the Department of Commerce) significantly controlled the foreign trade of the rebellious colonies and was responsible for distributing supplies to the army and to the colonies. Because the Secret Committee granted numerous contracts to the firm of Willing and Morris, as well as to associates and relatives of Morris's friend, Silas Deane of Connecticut, mutterings that chicanery was rampant soon were heard from John and Sam Adams and the Lees of Virginia, a faction almost relentlessly suspicious of Washington, Franklin, John Jay, and Thomas Jefferson. The mutterings, growing louder and more insistent with time, eventually would embroil Morris in a vicious controversy.

The Committtee of Secret Correspondence (later the Committee for Foreign Affairs and the seed of the Department of State) was appointed "for the sole purpose of corresponding with our friends in Great Britain, Ireland, and other parts of the world." The committee could act on its own initiative and hire whatever agents it needed. Its chief goal, of course, was to discover to what extent foreign powers, notably France, were inclined to support the rebellion.

These were only two of the committees on which Morris was a driving force. He was also a member of the Marine Committee, a group charged with establishing a colonial navy. Together with John Adams, Benjamin Harrison, and two others, he was appointed "to consider of the fortifying one or more ports on the American Coast, in the strongest manner for the Protection of our Cruisers. . . ." By himself Morris was commissioned to negotiate bills of exchange and to take other measures to obtain money for the impoverished Congress and army.

Morris, despite his zeal in performing his duties, had strong reservations about the path the colonies were taking. Like many others, he believed that defiance of injustice was one matter, but that severing ties with Britain was quite another.

As Morris hurled himself energetically from one tiresome and time-consuming task to another, Congress continued its meetings throughout the spring of 1776 in a spacious, white-paneled room on the ground floor of the east end of the State House. The movement toward independence gained more and more supporters, many converted by the inflammatory arguments set forth by Tom Paine in *Common Sense,* which appeared in January, 1776. Those who urged reconciliation with Britain were heeded less and less. In April, North Carolina authorized its delegates to support "Independency." Soon Virginia was urging its delegates to take the lead in offering a resolution for independence; with alacrity Richard Henry Lee complied on June 7. His resolution contained three distinct points:

> That these United Colonies are, and of right ought to be, free and independent States, that they are absolved from all allegiance to the British Crown, and that all political connection between them and the State of Great Britain is, and ought to be, totally dissolved.
>
> That it is expedient forthwith to take the most effectual measures for forming foreign Alliances.
>
> That a plan of confederation be prepared and transmitted to the respective Colonies for their consideration and approbation.

A vigorous debate began, with delegates from Pennsylvania, New York, and South Carolina opposing the resolution, and John Adams notably outspoken in its support. On June 10 the conservatives won a point by gaining postponement of a formal vote for three weeks and lost a point in being forced to yield to the appointment of a committee to draft a Declaration of Independence, in case the vote should be affirmative. Benjamin Franklin of Pennsylvania, John Adams of Massachusetts, Robert Livingston of New York, Roger Sherman of Connecticut, and

Thomas Jefferson of Virginia were named to this committee. A second committee, with a member from each colony, was directed to draw up a plan of confederation. A third committee was designated to "prepare a plan of treaties to be proposed to foreign powers"—its members being Franklin, John Adams, John Dickinson, Benjamin Harrison, and Robert Morris.

July 1, the day appointed for the consideration of the resolution, was clear and scorching. The delegates met at the State House and resolved themselves into a "committee of the whole," a device by which any debate and vote could be regarded as unofficial. When the debate started, John Dickinson, author of the influential *Letters from a Farmer in Pennsylvania*, which had questioned Parliament's power to tax the colonies for revenue, began to speak slowly, judiciously, sincerely. The colonies, he argued, were unprepared for independence. They were poor and unable to support themselves.

Then John Adams rose to argue for independence. His speech was so persuasive and powerful that, when the unofficial vote was taken, nine of the thirteen colonies were in the affirmative. New York abstained, Delaware's vote was split between the two members present, and South Carolina and Pennsylvania voted against the resolution. The final—and formal—vote was deferred to the next day.

Although the Pennsylvania delegation voted as a unit, three of the seven members—Franklin, Morton, and Wilson—favored independence; and four—Morris, Willing, Dickinson, and Humphreys—opposed it. Although both Morris and Dickinson were unwilling to vote contrary to their beliefs, they decided that they would voluntarily absent themselves from the session on July 2, when the formal vote would be taken.

Squalls of rain battered the windows of the State House as the delegates assembled on July 2. Morris and Dickinson, true to their word, stayed away, and so the Pennsylvania delegation was counted in favor of the resolution. South Carolina changed her vote to the affirmative. Everyone thought that Delaware's vote would remain split between the two delegates present, but

A Reluctant Rebel—and a Victory Dearly Bought 31

at the last minute a third delegate, mud-spattered Caesar Rodney, having just finished an eighty-mile dash on horseback from Delaware, strode into the State House and broke the tie in favor of independence. New York, waiting instructions from a convention at home, abstained for the moment, but within two weeks voted in the affirmative.

Immediately after voting, Congress began considering the draft of the Declaration of Independence written by Thomas Jefferson. A few phrases were changed or added. The delegates struck out a passage blaming the slave trade solely on King George III and some passages considered overly hostile to the British people as a whole. But the document ratified on July 4 was essentially the Declaration of Independence as Jefferson had composed it. Then, John Hancock, President of Congress, with his customary bold flourish, signed the document, which also was authenticated by the secretary of Congress; the delegates as a whole would sign when an engrossed parchment copy had been prepared. But the news was carried posthaste to all corners of the new United States of America.

Robert Morris's stand had required courage. As he pointed out to an acquaintance, some of their compatriots felt that any mention of reconciliation sounded like "high treason against the state, and I believe they would sooner punish a man for this crime than for bearing arms against us." He had opposed the Declaration of Independence because he believed that it had caused division at a time when union was needed, that it would "neither promote the interest nor redound to the honour of America."

July 20 had been set as the day to elect new delegates to represent Pennsylvania in Congress. Of the four delegates who had opposed the Declaration of Independence, only Morris was re-elected; his fellow Pennsylvanians, aware of his daring, energy, and efficiency, recognized that he was a public servant too rare to be easily replaced.

Morris viewed his re-election with little joy. Molly and the children had been complaining of neglect, and, although his account books could not reproach him with words or glances, they too demanded attention. Although Robert was tempted to decline his reappointment, he could not ignore the conviction that first had led him into public service and would lead him there again: each individual has the duty "to act his part in whatever station his country may call him to in hours of difficulty, danger, and distress." As he stated to an acquaintance, even though Congress had chosen a course contrary to his judgment and wishes, "I think that the individual who declines the service of his country because its councils are not conformable to his ideas makes but a bad subject; a good one will follow, if he cannot lead."

By August 2, the day when the engrossed parchment copy of the Declaration of Independence was read for the signatures of the delegates, the heat of the Philadelphia summer had become almost intolerable. As the delegates assembled in the chamber in the State House, many felt that they would be cooler in a kiln. The men present that day were not, in every instance, the men who had voted for or against independence a month earlier. Some of those present, like John and Sam Adams, were exultant. Some, like Abraham Clark of New Jersey, would soon wonder whether the fate in store for the signers was "freedom or a halter." Some, like Robert Morris, despite their reservations about the wisdom of the Declaration, threw all their considerable energies into making independence a reality.

Some of Robert's energies had to be diverted to aid his half brother, Thomas Wise Morris, now in his mid-twenties. Tom had grown increasingly wild, but Robert refused to abandon him. The older brother had done everything he could for the younger. As soon, Robert said, as "I fixed myself in the world . . . I took charge of this brother. I gave him the best education that could be obtained in Philadelphia, and . . . I took him into my counting-house." There Tom remained for about three years, but Robert was forced to send him to Spain to break his connections with worthless companions. Eventually Tom returned to America, and, Robert reported, he briefly "had great satisfaction in him." But Tom's former associates sought him out and once again were leading him astray.

Once again Robert sent Tom traveling in Europe and this time entrusted him with some business for Willing and Morris. No sooner had Tom arrived than Silas Deane reported that "the company he dipp'd at once into was so dissolute and expensive that it very essentially injured the reputation of your house, of which he was considered as being a member." Tom's escapades soon would cause Morris major embarrassment.

In late 1776, when Benjamin Franklin sailed from Philadelphia with the document appointing Silas Deane, Arthur Lee, and himself as commissioners to the court of France, he also bore Tom Morris's appointment as the Secret Committee's "Superentending Agent over all their European Concerns." Tom was empowered to purchase goods for Congress and to sell all consignments from Congress. Willing and Morris also intrusted him with "a good deal of Private business." Whether public business or private business, Tom handled it with equal irresponsibility.

More perilous problems loomed closer to home. Independence still had to be won. Victory after victory was being gained by the redcoats under General William Howe and the British fleet under his brother, Admiral Lord Richard Howe. The war, once so remote from Philadelphia, loomed closer and closer. The shabby, hungry Continental army was driven off Long Island; New York City fell to the redcoats. Early in December, Philadelphia was alarmed by news that Howe's army was at New Brunswick and proceeding toward the Delaware River. Many of the townspeople frantically began loading clothing, bedding, and furniture on wagons, ready for flight. Hordes of sick and wounded soldiers staggered into town.

The British now were too close for Congress's comfort. The delegates, with little dignity but great disorder, fled to Baltimore on December 12. Three members—so Congress thought—would remain behind in Philadelphia in charge of its affairs: Robert Morris and George Clymer of Pennsylvania, and George Walton of Georgia. Clymer and Walton vanished almost immediately, and Morris was left with the sole responsibility of conducting official affairs in the beleaguered former capital.

His activity was prodigious. Almost daily letters went to President John Hancock in Baltimore, to George Washington with the Continental army, to Benjamin Franklin, Silas Deane, and Arthur Lee, the American commissioners in France. Morris supervised the building of the city's defenses and spurred on the men—most of them volunteers drawn from the few dauntless citizens remaining in Philadelphia—in the shipyards constructing vessels for the Continental navy; he hoped to send six vessels to sea "if General Howe will give me but a few days more, and Lord Howe keep away his mighty myrmidons." Morris informed Congress that the Quaker City was "the greatest scene of distress that you can conceive." Only a small group of inhabitants remained—a few workmen, some Quakers, wounded soldiers, and a handful of able-bodied but ill-clothed troops that did what they could to help Morris with the city's defenses.

One source of relief was that he had sent Molly, Hetty, and the three boys to the home of Molly's stepsister, Sophia Hall, in Maryland. Just before Christmas a letter from Molly reported that they were "safely housed in this hospitable mansion." The journey had been especially hazardous because five-year-old Tom was afflicted with "a boil of an uncommon nature, and required the surgeon's hand." But the "greatest conflict," Molly said, was "flying from home." She longed to see her husband so that she could tell him all the details of the journey; writing a letter was unsatisfactory because "neither my patience nor paper will hold out."

Molly had expressed apprehension about losing household goods that she and the children had with them; Morris himself was dismayed that he had "many thousand pounds worth of effects here without any prospect of saving them." But, with characteristic determination, he announced, "I have throughout the alarm been determined not to quit until fairly done off."

Once Morris found himself in an executive position he minced no words about the inefficiency, mismanagement, and downright foolishness threatening to bankrupt the business Congress was attempting—the achieving of independence. To Franklin, Deane, and Lee he wrote that "so long as that august body [Congress] persist in the attempt to execute as well as to deliberate on their business, it will never be done as it ought and this has been urged many and many a time by myself and others, but some of them do not like to part with power and pay others for doing what they cannot do themselves." He justly pointed out to the commissioners that the colonists "knew not the hardships and calamities of war when they so boldly dared Britain to arms. Every man was then a bold patriot, felt himself equal to the contest, and seemed to wish for an opportunity of evincing his prowess." But now that the engagement had enmeshed the nation, Morris added, "when death and ruin stare us in the face, and when nothing but the most intrepid courage can rescue us from contempt and disgrace, sorry am I to say it, many of those who were foremost in noise shrink cowardlike from the danger, and are begging pardon without striking a blow."

He warned Congress that "Continental currency keeps losing its credit. Many people refuse openly and avowedly to receive it." Soon he cautioned, "If Congress mean to succeed in this contest, they must pay good executive men to do their business as it ought to be done, and not lavish millions away by their own mismanagement."

Morris could not confine himself, as he had planned, simply to naval affairs and the affairs of the Secret Committee. On all sides he heard complaints and confusion, so that he was forced to deal with concerns not actually under his authority. "Circumstanced as our affairs now are," he said, "I conceive it better to take Liberty's and assume some powers than to let the general interest suffer."

Luck occasionally was good. A few days before Christmas the *Andrew Doria,* sailing from St. Eustatius, successfully ran the British blockade of the Delaware River and arrived in port. Not only did she provide an additional desperately needed ship for the tiny navy, she also brought a desperately needed cargo: muskets, pistols, powder, as well as blankets, stockings, and jackets. Morris immediately distributed some of the supplies to the army camps; other supplies he prudently stored for future use in depots he established inland at Lancaster and elsewhere. Washington was profoundly concerned with obtaining "warm and comfortable Cloathing" to encourage reenlistments; he told Morris that "you may as well attempt to stop the Winds from blowing, or the Sun in its diurnal, as the Regiments from going when their term is expired."

Even more cheering than the arrival of the *Andrew Doria* was word of Washington's victorious assault on the Hessians at Trenton the day after Christmas, a victory which meant that, at least for the moment, Philadelphia was safe from attack. Shortly before the assault Washington had warned Morris that General Howe waited for only two occurrences before beseiging the Quaker City: "Ice for a Passage, and the dissolution of the poor remains of our debilitated Army." When the news reached Molly in Maryland, she wrote expressing fervent hope that Washington would succeed completely in routing "that impious army who from no other principle but that of enslaving this once happy country have prosecuted this cruel war."

But the victory did not mean that the indefatigable Morris could relax his exertions. On December 30 and again the next day Washington sent dispatches beseeching money—money to pay spies, money for provisions, money to provide each soldier with a bonus of ten dollars if he would continue for another month. Washington urged Morris to borrow money upon the merchant's private credit: "every Man of Interest and every Lover of his Country must strain his Credit upon such an Occasion."

Morris's response was in character: "I mean to borrow silver, and promise payment in gold, and then collect the gold in the best manner I can." This policy, which often worked miraculously when Morris was exerting himself in the public interest, would prove treacherous when he applied it to his private interests.

With feverish activity he scraped together what hard money he could find: English crowns and shillings, French half crowns, Spanish milled dollars. He begged from the few wealthy Quakers who were not Loyalists and who had not fled when Congress took flight. One story says that the following dialogue occurred when Morris knocked at a neighbor's door:

"What news so early, Robert?"

"The news is just this, my friend. General Washington needs a certain sum of hard money, and I must send it to him immediately. I would like you to lend me $50,000."

"But what is thy security, Robert, for this large sum?"

"My word and my honor."

"Thou shalt have it."

Morris dispatched the money with a letter to Washington early on New Year's Day, 1777. He had some difficulty in finding a messenger, he said, because "none concerned in this movement except myself are up. I shall rouse them immediately." Then he added, "If further occasional supplies of money are necessary, you may depend on my exertions either in a public or private capacity."

Morris was playing a desperate and dangerous game for the benefit of his country. If the British entered the city before he could flee, the Loyalists—of whom Philadelphia had a goodly share—would betray him immediately. Even more dangerous was his often being forced to act without authority from Congress, acts that aroused the jealousy and suspicion of his fellow congressmen, safe if not comfortable in Baltimore. Increasingly he had cause to mingle his private funds and private credit with public funds. In such perilous moments few protested, but the time would come when his integrity would be vehemently and viciously challenged.

The funds Morris sent reached Washington just as he was preparing to clash with the British at Princeton. There, on January 3, 1777, the Continental army drove the redcoats under Cornwallis back to New Brunswick. Then, having cleared the enemy from all but the easternmost part of New Jersey, Washington pulled his battered forces into winter quarters at Morristown.

When Molly heard of the victory at Princeton, her reaction was similar to that which many must have felt. On January 15, she wrote her husband:

> I wish to make myself as agreeable as possible to this family, and as they had invited a party of young folk to a Twelfth Cake, I tryed to be cheerful; how could I be really so when hourly in expectation of hearing the determination of so important a Battle, and when the express arrived and pronounced Washington victorious, would you believe it, your Molly could not join in the general rejoicing? No! nor never can at a victory so dearly bought.

IV

The Fall of a City and of a "Worthless Wretch"

"If you wish to please your friends, come soon to us," Benjamin Harrison wrote Robert Morris from Baltimore, "but if you desire to keep out of the damnedest hole in the world come not here. . . . In this infernal sink . . . there is not even a tavern that one can turn to for exercise and amusement." Fat and profane, Benjamin Harrison nevertheless reflected the attitude of most congressmen toward the temporary capital.

During the early months of 1777, Robert Morris scarcely had time for sleep, let alone trips to Baltimore. The commissioners in France had made an agreement to supply tobacco in exchange for stores and supplies. Although Morris succeeded in obtaining thousands of hogsheads of tobacco, vessels in which to ship them were almost impossible to secure. Because none was available in the South, where the tobacco was, Morris had to buy or charter ships in New England and send them south. Some of the ships sent to France with tobacco and other cargoes were captured by the British; the cargoes of other ships were commandeered for Washington's army before the vessels could sail from the colonies. At Philadelphia, as Morris wrote to Silas Deane, "We were blocked up the best part of the Season and lost several valuable Cargoes intended for you."

Few supplies from Deane were reaching Morris in Philadelphia. Morris suggested to Deane that "you may have leisure to repent hereafter that you missed so fine an opportunity of making a Fortune. The prices of all imported articles have been enormously high. . . . there is plenty of room to make as much money as you please."

This statement reflects an attitude that eventually would open both Morris and Deane to attack. A strict code of ethics had not yet been formulated about conflict of interests. Morris—and other members of the Continental Congress as well—considered themselves justified in indulging in private enterprises and making profits at the same time (and often through the same channels) that they were conducting business on behalf of Congress. On more than one occasion Morris shipped goods for Willing and Morris in a ship whose insurance and expenses were paid by Congress; his justification was that he paid the going rates for freight. At one point twenty ships owned by Willing and Morris —and five more in which the firm owned a share—were transporting cargoes for the Secret Committee and simultaneously carrying goods for the firm's private business. Morris himself had agents in the South to keep produce flowing to the North, and agents in New England to market his imports; in the Middle Atlantic states he almost dominated the export-import commerce. Moreover, his trading vessels kept him in close communication with Europe and with the West Indies.

Martinique provided a friendly haven where Continental vessels could be refitted, repaired, and provisioned. In June, 1776, Congress had sent bright, enterprising, twenty-four-year-old William Bingham of Philadelphia there to function as its commercial agent. Bingham already had seen service as secretary of the Committee of Secret Correspondence. Bingham also was to serve as agent for Willing and Morris. Robert gave the young man some characteristic advice: "when cargoes arrive one way or tother the profitts are ever so great. It is well worth risquing largely for one arrival will pay for two, three, or four losses. Therefore its best to keep doing something constantly." Bingham took Morris's advice to heart; when the young merchant returned to Philadelphia in mid-1780, he was a wealthy man, and he became wealthier by marrying Thomas Willing's daughter Anne.

In addition to his duties for Congress and Willing and Morris, Bingham kept sending Morris French volunteers for service in the Continental army. The flood grew so overwhelming that Morris finally pleaded with him "to spare me all you can in the Introduction of French Officers to me . . . could I speak the Language and had spare time it woud be a pleasure but it is now too much the reverse. . . . really they are flocking over in such Numbers from every Port by every Ship that I don't know what we shall do with them."

Bingham, authorized by Congress to "encourage as many private adventurers as you can," actively began arming merchant ships, generally manned by Frenchmen, to engage in buccaneering, one of the most expeditious ways to provide himself and his sponsors with cash and cargoes. Although Robert Morris at first opposed privateering, as the war progressed and the demands for hard money became more insistent than ever, he changed his mind. Early in 1777 he confessed to Bingham, "I have seen much Rapine Plunder & Destruction . . . executed on the Americans that I join you in thinking it a Duty to oppose & distress so Merciless an Enemy in every shape we can. . . ."

During all these commercial ventures—on behalf of the Secret Committee and on behalf of Willing and Morris—Robert did his best to keep his accounts in order. But the task was almost insuperable. The fate of ships and cargoes frequently was uncertain for months, sometimes years. When vessels were captured or sunk, invoices disappeared. And, above all, lines of communication often were snarled or broken.

Morris's concern with the Continental navy also kept him scurrying during this winter and early spring of 1777. From Baltimore, where Congress still was uncomfortably conducting its business, President John Hancock wrote to him:

I admire the spirited conduct of little Jones; pray push him out again. I know he does not love to be idle, & I am as certain you wish him to be constantly active, he is a fine fellow & he shall meet with every notice of mine & I am confident you will join me.

"Little Jones" was twenty-nine-year-old Captain John Paul Jones, the hazel-eyed, brown-haired Scots sailor who stood about five-and-a-half feet tall. Early in February, Morris, acting for Congress, ordered Jones to take command of five vessels to harass British possessions in the West Indies and Florida. First, Jones was to seize the cannon and supplies at St. Christopher in the West Indies. Then, after alarming Jamaica by putting in at some of its ports, he was to sail to Pensacola on the Gulf of Mexico, where he was to capture the town, some British sloops, and a hundred or more pieces of artillery. From Pensacola a portion of his fleet was to cruise along the mouth of the Mississippi River and attack British merchantmen coming down the river with valuable cargoes. Finally, he was to raise an alarm at St. Augustine.

Morris hoped these tactics would force the British to withdraw vessels from the coast of the United States in order to defend their besieged territory. Although the expedition never was carried out—for reasons over which Morris and Jones had no control—the strategy Morris proposed would undoubtedly have proved more beneficial than the destruction of commerce on which the Continental navy expended much of its energy.

During these early months of 1777, Morris, who had been re-elected to Congress but not to the Pennsylvania Assembly, kept up a constant correspondence with Washington in the Continental army's winter quarters in the hills near Morristown, New Jersey. Washington would ask Morris to do what he could about increasing production at the Philadelphia foundry for casting brass cannon. Or he would ask Morris to send him "a pound or two of good Sealing Wax if it is to be procured."

The two usually were concerned with more important matters than sealing wax. In a letter to Washington, Morris lamented that, certain members having resigned from Congress, no new delegates had been appointed by the various states to take their place: "What is to become of America and its cause, if a constant fluctuation is to take place among its Counsellors . . . ?" Again he wrote to condemn the practice of short enlistments and to inveigh against the "harpies" who "get their livings by feeding and entertaining" the soldiers:

> They keep the fellows drunk while the money holds out; when it is gone, they encourage them to reenlist for the sake of bounty, then to drinking again; that bounty gone, and more money still wanted, they must enlist again with some other officer, receive a fresh bounty and get more drunk, &c. This scene is actually carrying on here daily, and does immense injury to the recruiting service.

The ever-increasing burden of overwork was taking its toll. "The Congress give me too many employments & heap vastly too much on me for any man living to do as it shou'd be," he said. "If they had left me to manage their Commercial matters & those only I cou'd have done great things, but instead of that all their active business is pushed on me. . . ." About the same time he notified Washington that "I have been attacked by a weakness in my eyes, and writing is the most dangerous thing I can do whilst it continues." But he kept on writing.

Others, in addition to George Washington, realized the strain under which Morris worked as essentially the sole representative of the government in Philadelphia. Near the end of February, the danger from Howe's army apparently past, Congress made plans to return from Baltimore to the Quaker City. President John Hancock wrote to Morris, "I hope our coming there will in some degree relieve you from the great burden that has laid upon you. No money, constant application for it, and a steady succession of business to attend to has made your situation hard indeed."

On March 12, with a quorum assembled in the State House, Congress resumed its sessions. By April 8 every state was represented, and debates were being held on the Articles of Confederation, which had first been presented to Congress in July, 1776.

The greatest joy for Robert Morris was not that Congress had returned, but that his wife and four children were back with him. The rigorous winter had taken its toll of Molly, as it had of her husband. In mid-March she wrote to her mother in Maryland, "I suppose Jemmy Hall has told you how everybody exclaims at my thinness; several of my acquaintance did not know me till they had time to recollect, and then declared there was very little traces of my former self." In this letter she proudly informed her mother that Congress had chosen her brother, William White, as chaplain.

The career of Robert's half brother, Tom, was increasingly causing shame, not pride. In January, Robert expressed concern about Tom—and attempted to defend him—in a letter to Silas Deane:

> He had been Frolicksome & Foolish many times as a Boy, but as I never knew him to depart from Principles of honor and Integrity in his wildest days, I never entertained a doubt of his becoming an excellent Character in the progress of his Manhood; these considerations, and the good accounts given of him by all my Friends in Spain and Italy, induced me not only to commit to his care my own private Business in which he is a Partner, but to recommend him to the Superintendency of the Public business, as you will have seen heretofore; and I know also that he has good Mercantile Abilitys, if he will but exercise them properly . . . . it will make me most unhappy if the Public business should have suffered by this Appointment.

By the end of June public letters from the commissioners fully had exposed Tom's misconduct. Robert wrote angrily to Deane:

> These letters arrived long before I had a scrip of a Pen from you on the subject. It occurred to me instantly that I had unbosomed myself to you respecting him; that I had Sollicited your Friendship

in his favour, and asked you to inform me fully and freely of his Conduct; that to all this I never had a word in answer, and found your name at the bottom of Letters blasting his character in the most Public manner, and exposing me to feelings the most Poignant I ever knew.

Deane, defending himself vigorously against Morris's charges, wrote that he had acted from disinterested motives. He added that "no private concern affects me more, than having drawn on myself your resentment of my desire of serving you. Be assured that I retain the highest esteem and respect for you in your public as well as private character, and am your sincere friend."

Deane, Franklin, and Lee were not alone in their censure of Tom Morris. A friend wrote John Adams that Tom was "Drunk at least Twentytwo Hours of every Twentyfour.... He neglects all business because he has rendered himself incapable of any. In short, I never saw a man in a more deplorable situation."

While the controversy about Tom Morris raged, the scene of the war moved closer and closer to Philadelphia. Toward the end of July, 1777, General Howe embarked with his troops from New York, sailed to the Chesapeake, and landed his men scarcely fifty-five miles from the capital at Philadelphia. Washington's army moved south to meet the British; on Sunday, August 24, starting at seven o'clock in the morning, about ten thousand soldiers paraded through Philadelphia, down Front Street, up Chestnut, turning toward the Common, and then on. Pathetic attempts were made to spruce up the tattered troops, most without uniforms. Each soldier bore a sprig of green, and the drums and fifes were commanded to play "with such moderation that the man may step ... without dancing along or totally disregarding the music, which has been too often the case." John Adams, writing to his wife, noted, "Our soldiers have not yet quite the air of soldiers. They don't step exactly in time. They don't hold their heads quite erect, nor turn out their toes so exactly as they ought." Indeed, he added, "They don't all of them cock their hats; and such as do, don't all wear them the same way."

Washington took up his position on the eastern side of Brandywine Creek, not far from Wilmington, and on September 11, Howe and his forces attacked, forced the American army back toward Philadelphia, and by September 26 had occupied the Quaker City.

On September 19 Congress fled to Lancaster. Robert Morton, a young Philadelphia Loyalist, observed in his diary that word of Howe's approach toward the Schuylkill "so much alarmed the Gentlemen of the Congress, the military officers, and other friends to the general cause of American freedom and independence, that they decamped with the utmost precipitation, and in the greatest confusion. . . ." The movement to Lancaster, Congressman Thomas Burke of North Carolina said, "was not by a Vote but by universal Consent, for every Member Consulted his own Particular Safety."

The harried members of Congress paused at Lancaster only long enough to hold one session. "Hearts were still fluttering in some bosoms," one congressman said, and so the representatives fled on to York, where a greater distance and the broad Susquehanna River lay between them and Howe's forces. "Here," a member said early in October, when they had settled down at York, "we are at least sufficiently *retired* and can deliberate without interruption."

Early on the morning of October 4, Washington's troops confronted the British at Germantown, but were forced to withdraw to the northwest to an insignificant village at the junction of Valley Creek and the Schuylkill River. There, at Valley Forge, the weary, hungry Continental army pitched camp on a windswept wooded hillside on December 18. This bleak site was to be Washington's winter quarters.

When Congress had rushed pell-mell out of Philadelphia, Robert Morris conveyed his family—now increased by the birth of a son Charles on July 11—up the turnpike to Lancaster. Having taken only what they valued most from their town house and from "The Hills," they moved in a caravan of covered wagons to a village about ten miles from Lancaster named Manheim, built by the eccentric German immigrant, the self-styled Baron Stiegel, and noted for its glassworks. The Morrises took refuge in "The Castle," the home built by Stiegel—and a palatial refuge it was. The walls were covered with tapestries, the woodwork was richly carved, and the furnishings were imposing.

During this winter at York and at Manheim, Robert Morris had more worries than those about his half brother. A letter from Tench Tilghman written November 29 brought disheartening news: "I had a view of your Country seat a few days ago from the west side of the Schuylkill. The soil is not destroyed but in every other respect it is in a state of Nature . . . every House from Mr. Dickensons to yours is either burnt or what is as bad pulled to pieces."

The sessions that Congress had resumed seemed more like squabbles. The debate raged over the Articles of Confederation. Morris wrote to General Gates, commanding the Continental troops in New York State, "We are disputing about liberties, privileges, posts, and places, at the very time we ought to have nothing in mind but the securing of those objects and placing them on such a footing as to make them worth contending for amongst overselves hereafter." Gates's maneuvers soon brought Congress encouraging news when word arrived that his troops had achieved a glorious triumph at Saratoga over the British general, "Gentleman Johnny" Burgoyne.

When Congress fled, Thomas Willing had remained in Philadelphia to keep the business and his property from being confiscated by the British. Through him General Howe sent notice to the citizens of Philadelphia that they would not be molested when the British troops entered the city. The entry of the smartly uniformed redcoats and the Hessian grenadiers in green and yellow was uneventful. Howe appointed Loyalist Joseph Galloway as civilian head of the city; when Howe sent Galloway to Willing with an oath of allegiance, the merchant refused to sign.

Willing almost immediately had to combat a widespread rumor of the firm's financial instability. "Curse on the malice of those who have invented it," Willing wrote to his partner. "I hope like the viper in the path, they will find yet a file to gnaw, which may break their teeth. The time may again come, when some of them may court our favours."

Although Morris had made enemies, he also had made stalwart friends, among them John Hancock, who sent the following note on October 25: "Mr. H. observing that Mr. Morris frequently walks with a cane, takes the freedom to Send him a Gold Head for a Cane, of which he requests Mr. Morris's acceptance, as a small token of his Reel Regard & friendship for him." Hancock, having requested a leave of absence from Congress, was about to set behind him the trials and tribulations of the presidency of Congress to return to Boston to tend to his personal affairs. Reportedly Morris was offered the presidency, but declined because of the pressure of other responsibilities. Indeed, on November 11, Morris himself requested a six-months' leave to straighten out private and public matters.

The long, acrimonious debate over the Articles of Confederation was drawing to a close. On November 15 the thirteen Articles were formally adopted by Congress, signed by the delegates, Morris among them, and two days later were sent to each state for prompt ratification—a process that took more than three years.

Before leaving Congress, Morris volunteered to take home with him the account books of the Secret Committee and to devote his spare time to an attempt to bring order to the confused records; the books were not actually delivered to him at Manheim until the end of December. Morris, on his last day in Congress, was appointed with two other delegates to visit Washing-

The Fall of a City and of a "Worthless Wretch" 49

ton at Valley Forge to urge him to conduct a winter campaign against the British in Philadelphia—a mission that took about two weeks and failed to persuade Washington to attempt what would have been a foolhardy venture.

While at Manheim, Morris received a perplexing visit from a former employee, John Brown, sent on to him by Willing. Brown purported to carry a message from General Howe, a guarantee that if Congress would rescind the Declaration of Independence, he would withdraw the British army and fleet and restore the status of 1763. Learning of the message, the Pennsylvania Council of Safety seized Brown and hustled him off to jail; his proposal smacked of sedition. Indeed, Congress had passed resolutions declaring that discussing terms with the enemy was a traitorous action. Morris fearlessly interceded, swearing that Brown's intentions were innocent, urging that Brown be paroled in his custody. Apparently Brown lay in jail for almost two months; not until January 25, 1778, was he freed on bail, with the restriction that he not go more than five miles from Manheim.

Morris was having less luck interceding for his wastrel half brother, Tom. Late in September, 1777, Silas Deane wrote from Paris:

> Your brother's conduct cannot at this time be a secret in America. . . . The friends of America in France, as well as the Americans themselves, are so surprised to find him still continued in the most important, as well as the most delicate trust, and of being at the head as it were of the American commerce at this critical period, and at the same time are grieved to see the effects this confidence has on him. You may suppose that this occasions much speculation, not among the Americans only, but among the merchants of Europe, to whom the management of our affairs in the commercial department is no secret. . . . I fear the part you have taken for your brother in this affair, though you have doubtless acted from the most natural as well as generous and good principles, may produce consequences which none but your as well as my enemies wish for. . . .

Less than two weeks later Deane reported a disgraceful incident. Toward the end of September, Tom, bearing a worn, dirty letter from Robert, had called on Deane and insisted that Deane accompany him to Benjamin Franklin's residence. There Tom berated the two commissioners, accused them of villifying him to Congress, insisted that Congress supported him, and swore that he would ever afterwards despise them and treat them with the utmost contempt.

According to Deane, Dr. Franklin replied, "It gives me great pleasure to be respected by men who are themselves respectable, but I am indifferent to the sentiments of those of a different character, and I only wish that your future conduct may be such as to entitle you to the approbation of your honorable constituents."

On parting, Tom insisted that he would show Robert's letter, which expressed sympathy for him, to anyone he could find to read it. Deane confided to Robert that he was apprehensive "that many who are neither friends to him [Tom] nor to America may already have seen it, and that this indiscreet exposure of it may give our enemies an opportunity of using it to strengthen their accounts of our internal divisions, animosities, &c."

Robert no longer could overlook—or attempt to defend—the behavior of his half brother. The day after Christmas, 1777, he wrote a lengthy letter to Henry Laurens, President of Congress, to be read aloud before the delegates, a letter in which he explained his attempts to redeem Tom, attempts which repeatedly failed. Robert now requested that Tom be dismissed from his position of trust, a trust he had betrayed. In closing, Robert remarked, "My distress is more than I can describe; to think that in the midst of the most ardent exertions I was capable of making to promote the interest and welfare of my country, I should be the means of introducing a worthless wretch to disgrace and discredit it is too much to bear."

Tom Morris was not to prove a disgrace to his country and to his half brother much longer. Taken ill in Nantes, he died at five o'clock in the morning of January 31, 1778. Among those attending his funeral was Captain John Paul Jones, who was refitting the *Ranger* at Nantes, just prior to his notable exploits in April in the Irish Sea and at Whitehaven, England, where he spiked the guns of the fort and set fire to a ship at anchor. Somewhat ironically, during the funeral the *Ranger* fired a salute of thirteen minute-guns in honor of Tom Morris, the "worthless wretch."

V

Hard Cash and a Hard-fought Campaign

The threat Tom Morris's actions posed to the American cause in France proved negligible. By mid-February, 1778, two treaties of alliance had been signed between France and the United States. Robert Morris was exultant. "We are at the height of our joy here," Morris remarked in a letter to William Bingham on May 5. "You may set it down as a certainty that Great Britain has lost America and that these states are free and independent."

Three days later Sir Henry Clinton replaced General Howe in Philadelphia and, worried by reports of a French fleet sailing toward America, decided to consolidate British forces by evacuating the Quaker City and returning to New York City. In June the British fleet sailed down the Delaware River, and by the eighteenth the last detachment of redcoats had marched out of town. The next day General Benedict Arnold paraded jauntily into the capital to establish an American military government. Washington moved his forces northward across New Jersey; after an indecisive battle at Monmouth, the Continentals entrenched themselves at White Plains, slightly to the north of New York City.

Congress was not long in following the troops into Philadelphia. The delegates, discovering that the British had left the State House filthy and sordid, held their sessions in College Hall. Many of the homes in the city had been vandalized; some had been used as stables, with holes cut in the drawing room floors to remove the manure. Trees had been chopped down and fences demolished to provide the British with firewood. And the cemetery beside the Walnut Street prison had hundreds of new graves where ill-treated prisoners of the British lay buried.

At Manheim, Morris worked on the account books of the Secret Committee, spending, he said, "the little leisure which remained from my private avocations, and the many interruptions occasioned by public business, which pursued me into my retirement, and many times obliged me to visit York-town, each visit taking up from five to six days."

Early in June he spent some time with Washington at Valley Forge; following the evacuation of the British, he returned to Philadelphia for a week, then journeyed to Manheim to bring Molly back to "The Hills." The estate was in as deplorable a condition as Tilghman had reported. A friend commented, "I am really concerned for the dismantled condition of the Hills, tis but a pitiful kind of revenge to fall on houses and gardens for the offences of their owners, but such have been and ever will be the case with the low minded.'"

Morris's term in Congress expired on November 1, 1778; that same autumn he was elected to the Pennsylvania Assembly. More than one man lamented Morris's absence from the committees he had served so vigorously. As Captain Thomas Bell wrote to John Paul Jones, "Mr. Morris has left the Marien [the Marine Committee] and Every thing is Going to the devel as fast Can." But Molly Morris was delighted to have more of her husband's company than she had enjoyed for years. "We are gay," she wrote to her mother in November. "We have a great many balls and entertainments, and soon the Assemblys will begin." Molly was pregnant again; a daughter, Maria, was born on April 24, 1779.

Morris, however, occupied himself with thoughts of more than the Assembly balls. For two reasons he had decided to terminate his long partnership with Thomas Willing. The scandal about

Tom Morris's behavior had damaged the firm's credit, and Willing's persistence in remaining in the city during the British occupation had increasingly irritated Morris's sense of proper patriotic conduct. Within a few years he had involved himself in the astounding number of nine new partnerships, as well as in a multitude of less significant enterprises; eventually he would resume business relations with Willing.

But troubles were mustering. Early in 1778 his friend Silas Deane was recalled by Congress to find himself ferociously attacked, charged with mismanagement and even fraud. When Congress refused to let Deane meet his accusers and testify in person, he tried presenting his case through the public press, only to be outwitted at every turn of the pen by the master propagandist, Tom Paine. By April, 1778, John Adams had replaced Deane as a commissioner in France.

In January, 1779, Paine drew Morris into the dispute by charging that Morris had been negligent in settling his accounts for the Secret Committee; Paine implied that Morris had had ten months in which to bring order to the chaos. Morris asserted vigorously that the books had been his to work on little more than five months; moreover, he claimed, a balance was due from Congress to Willing and Morris, not *vice versa*. Henry Laurens of South Carolina then charged that Morris had dishonestly received compensation from public funds for a private loss, that of the *Farmer*, captured by the British in 1777. Congress immediately appointed a committee to investigate the charges. On February 15, 1779, John Jay, then President of Congress, sent Morris the committee's report, which exonerated him completely; he had acted "with fidelity and integrity and an honorable zeal for the happiness of his country."

General Thomas Mifflin, condemning the "rascally" attack, summed up in a letter the opinion of many: "Payne, like the enthusiastic Madman of the East, was determined to run the Muck—he sallied forth, stabbed three or four slightly, met with you but missing his Aim fell a victim to his own Stroke; and by attempting too much will enjoy a most mortifying and general contempt." Morris was undaunted by attacks by Paine and others. "I never came forth into Public Life on any other ground than a desire to promote and support the just & necessary opposition to the Tyranny of Great Britain," he said; ". . . whilst I have a share in the Public Councils . . . my Voice will always speak the dictates of my own. . . ."

No sooner had the controversy with Paine died down than Morris, together with other merchants, became embroiled in a dispute with the citizens of Philadelphia. Throughout the country prices of food were soaring, and bitter tempers soared with them. The situation had been made worse by the winter, the worst anyone could remember. In the spring of 1779 vessels arrived with cargoes of flour consigned to Morris and others. The public, assuming that the price would fall with the plentiful supply, became enraged when the price rose even higher than before. At a town meeting in the State House yard, a committee including David Rittenhouse, the astronomer; Charles Willson Peale, the artist; and Tom Paine was appointed to protest to Morris. Morris replied that the flour, bought for the French fleet, belonged to John Holker, "his Most Christian Majestys Agent"; Holker, confronted by the committee, announced that he would be held accountable only by Congress. Morris complained that, spurred on by the committee, housewives with empty sacks were besieging his office, demanding flour.

Two months later another town meeting erupted into a riot. When General John Cadwallader tried to defend Morris, a mob attacked him with clubs. The rabble, boarding outgoing ships, forced them back into port. Wheat was seized. Wagons leaving the city with coffee, tea, and sugar were turned back. The committee of citizens attempted to fix prices. Finally Congress was forced to intervene; Morris and other merchants published a resolution condemning mob rule.

That fall mob violence reached a zenith. Placards appeared throughout the city denouncing Morris, James Wilson, Thomas

Mifflin, and other conservatives. Hearing that Wilson's home, soon satirically called "Fort Wilson," was to be attacked, Morris, Mifflin, and others barricaded themselves with him. Wilson, a Scottish-born lawyer, had been one of the signers of the Declaration of Independence; he was a tall, dignified man, near-sighted, but with a mind that was "one blaze of light." Soon about two hundred men dragging two cannons marched up Walnut to Third, where Wilson's house stood. One of the besieged conservatives, a Captain Robert Campbell, opening a window, threatened the mob with a pistol. He was immediately shot dead. Both sides began firing. Some of the crowd tried to batter down the front door, but those inside barricaded the entrance.

The alarm spread swiftly throughout the city. Joseph Reed, president of the executive council of Pennsylvania, arrived at a gallop, his "knee buttons unfastened and his boots down," followed by troops. The mob scattered, but in the melee two were killed and many wounded. James Wilson was so shaken by the incident that he left town; Robert Morris went right on working.

The Pennsylvania radicals had not yet finished with Morris and Wilson. This faction, having gained control of the assembly and of the city government, charged that the College of Philadelphia was dominated by its undemocratic trustees, Morris, Wilson, and Willing among them. The assembly therefore repealed the College's charter and established a state institution, an act that almost destroyed one of the most liberal schools in America.

But Robert Morris hoped for tranquillity in 1780; no longer was he a member of Congress, and in the October elections he had not been returned to the Pennsylvania Assembly. By March, 1780, he could write to Benjamin Franklin, "My enemies, ashamed of their persecution, have quitted the pursuit, and I am in the peaceable possession of the most honourable station my ambition aspires to, that of a private citizen."

The rebuilding of "The Hills" already had started, and when Kitty Livingston visited the Morrises, she wrote to her sister,

Mrs. John Jay, "They have at present a delightful situation. . . . Mr. Morris has enlarged the buildings, converted the green-house into a dining-room, which far exceeds their expectations in beauty and convenience." Kitty had come to the Morrises because her father's home in New Jersey was considered unsafe; she enjoyed life with them so much that she stayed almost until the end of the war.

The war, during the first half of 1780, was catastrophic for the Americans. In South Carolina, Charleston fell to Sir Henry Clinton, and the Americans also suffered an overwhelming defeat at Camden. In New Jersey, Washington's camp at Morristown was the scene of a mutiny by unpaid, starving Connecticut soldiers. But July brought the Comte de Rochambeau and some six thousand French troops to Newport, Rhode Island, to aid the American cause.

Early in June a dedicated group of Philadelphians assembled to determine what they could do to relieve the national distress. Leading this group were the very men maligned by the radicals—Morris, Wilson, and Willing—as well as William Bingham, who had returned from Martinique. They determined to use their money and influence detested by the radicals—to establish a bank "for furnishing a supply of provisions for the armies of the United States." Robert Morris and Tench Francis, Jr., Willing's brother-in-law, were selected chairmen of the board of inspectors and shortly had raised £315,000 from subscribers, none of whom was allowed to gain any profit from the venture. Morris was one of three to subscribe £10,000. Congress gratefully agreed to cooperate, and the Pennsylvania Bank opened on July 17, 1780; it was ready to supply three million rations and three hundred hogsheads of rum to the Continental army. The bank was, Morris said, "nothing more than a patriotic subscription of continental money . . . for the purpose of purchasing provisions for a starving army." Morris's activities prompted young Alexander Hamilton to remark to a friend that Morris would be a good choice to head a department of finance: "He would have many things in his favor, and could, by his personal influence, give great weight to the measures he should adopt."

In the meantime Philadelphia had witnessed a growing romance between the military commander, Benedict Arnold, and one of the town's prettiest belles, Margaret Shippen. Back in November, 1778, Molly Morris had written to her mother, "Cupid has given our little General a more mortal wound than all the host of Britons could . . . Miss Peggy Shippen is the fair one." The thirty-nine-year-old Arnold and his nineteen-year-old bride, married in April, 1779, immediately started living beyond their means. Arnold, already under investigation for misconduct, was court-martialed in January, 1780, and, although acquitted of most charges, was sentenced to be reprimanded by Washington for two trivial offenses. The reprimand inflamed Arnold to seek revenge.

In mid-August the Morrises gave a dinner at their town house, a place described by a French visitor as "handsome, resembling perfectly the houses in London"; the Frenchman noted that the Morrises lived unostentatiously, but expensively, sparing "nothing which can contribute to his happiness and that of Mrs. Morris, to whom he is much attached." The dinner, the Morrises thought, would be an ordinary one, but a singular incident occurred. Among the guests was Peggy Shippen Arnold, whose husband had assumed command of West Point earlier that month. One of the guests, having heard that Arnold was to be promoted from the command at West Point to the command of the left wing of the army, congratulated Peggy on her husband's having been appointed to a more honorable command than West Point. Peggy, Morris later testified, was seized with "hysteric fits." The reason for her hysteria became tragically clear the following month. Arnold and Peggy had been concocting treasonable negotiations with the British General Clinton to deliver plans of the fortress and information about its weak points. The plot discovered, Arnold fled to safety aboard a British warship; his Philadelphia estate was confiscated; and Peggy was ordered to leave the city.

In October, having been re-elected to the Pennsylvania As-

From the collections of the Historical Society of Pennsylvania
Robert Morris, Sr. Artist unknown.

From the collections of the Historical Society of Pennsylvania
Mary White Morris. Engraving of a portrait by Peale.

Robert Morris. Portrait by Peale.

The London Coffee House. From Watson's *Annals of Philadelphia*, 1830.

Morris's home at 190 High Street, later the residence of Washington, and a view of the British barracks in Philadelphia. From Watson's *Annals of Philadelphia*, 1830.

Independence Hall. Drawn from an old print. From *Harper's Weekly*, July 8, 1876.

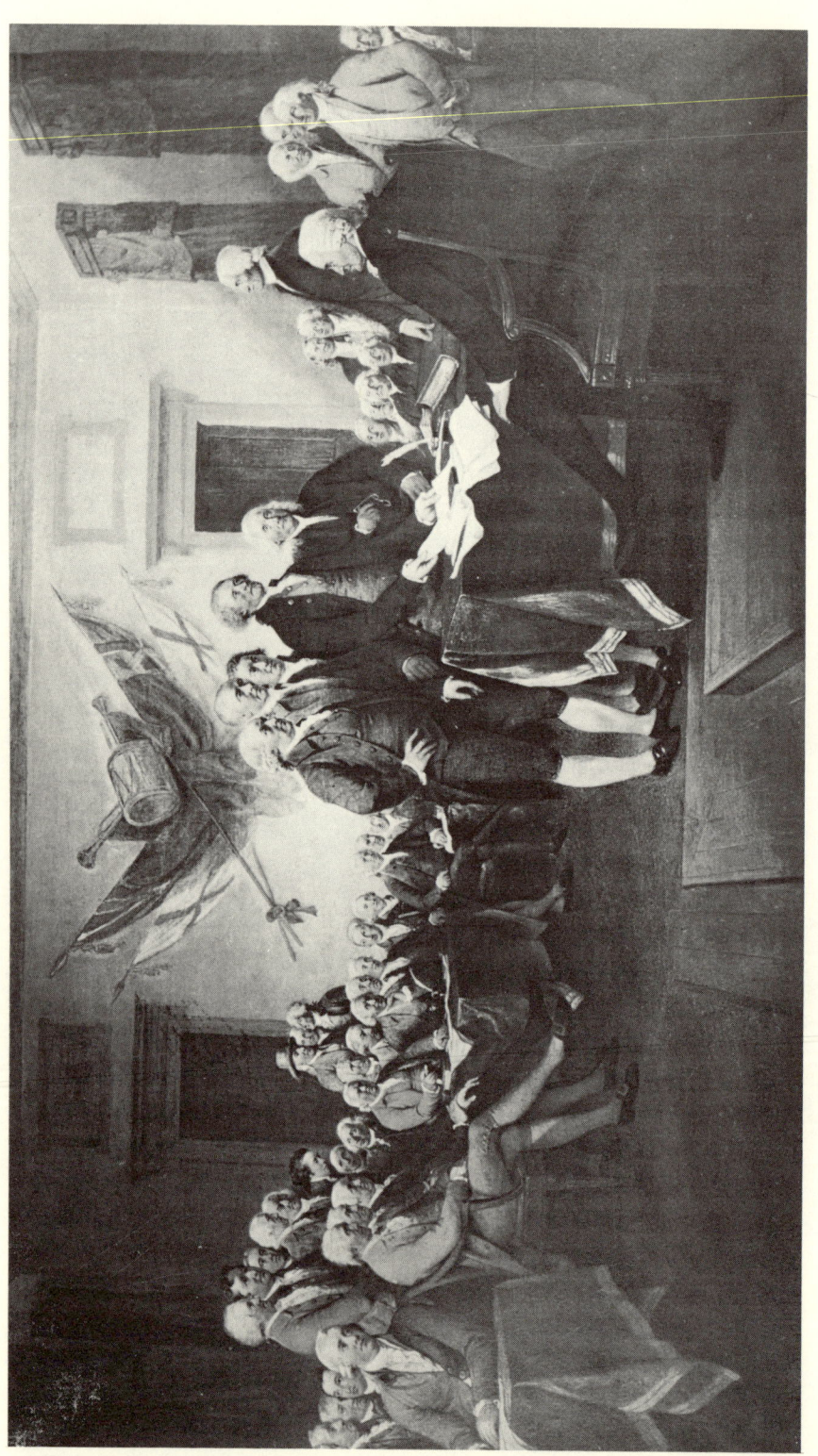

Signing of the Declaration of Independence. From the John Hancock Mutual Life Insurance Company's copy by Griswold Tyng of the painting by John Trumbull in the Yale University Art Gallery.

The Announcement of the Declaration of Independence. From the engraving by McGoffin.

Robert Morris. From the portrait by Chappel.

From the collections of the Historical Society of Pennsylvania

Painting by Woodside of "The home of Robert Morris, now known as 'Lemon Hill.'" Historians differ as to whether the building, "Lemon Hill," incorporates portions of Morris's "The Hills," which stood on the same site.

Mount Vernon. Engraving by Osborne.

Gouverneur Morris, 1780, by Pierre de Simitière.

Robert Morris. Oil miniature by Trumbull, 1790.

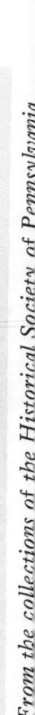

From the collections of the Historical Society of Pennsylvania

Gouverneur Morris. From the painting by Chappel.

Alexander Hamilton. From the painting by Chappel.

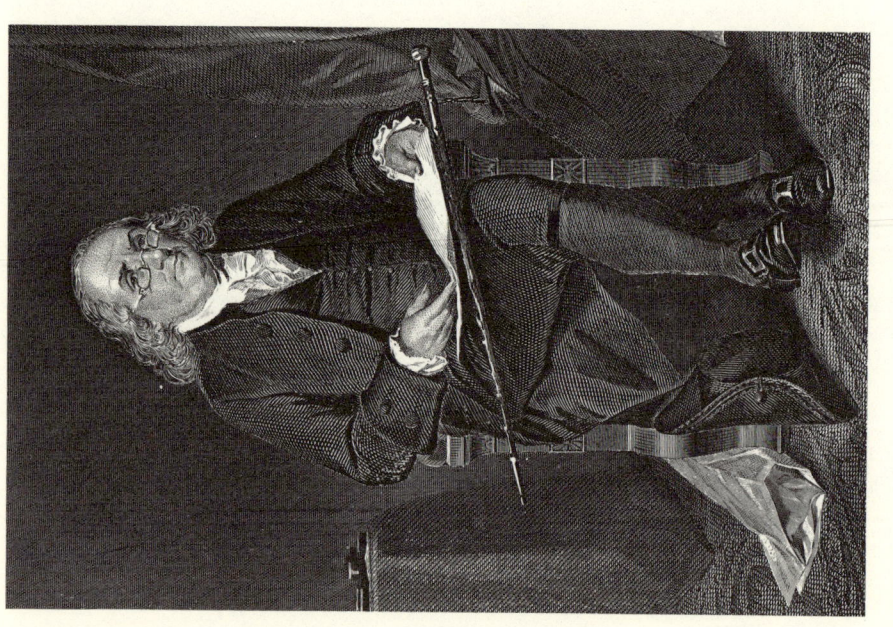

Benjamin Franklin. From the painting by Chappel.

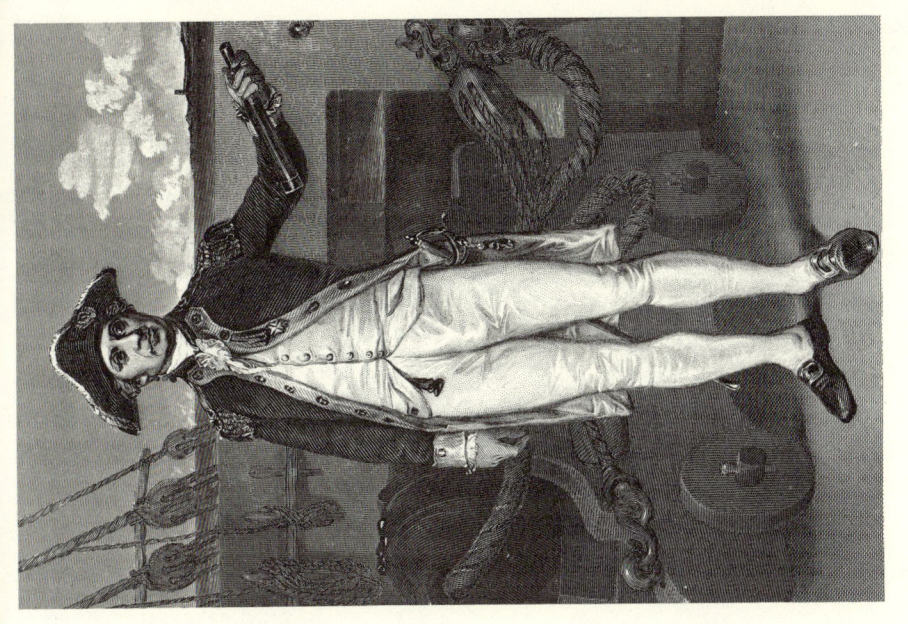

John Paul Jones, captain in the Continental navy. From the painting by Chappel.

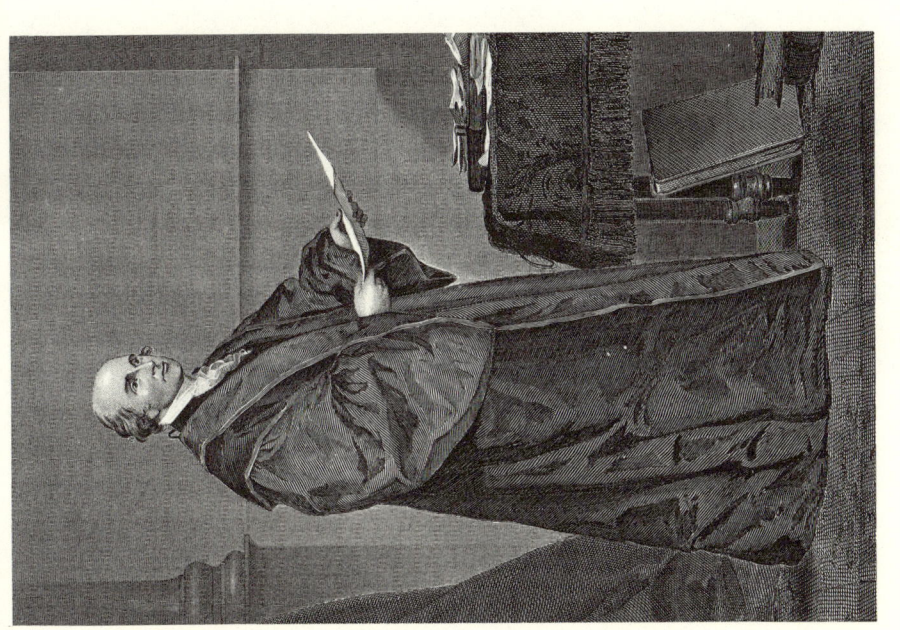

John Jay, first Chief Justice of the Supreme Court. From the painting by Chappel.

From the collections of the Historical Society of Pennsylvania
Robert Morris. Portrait by Otis and Sully.

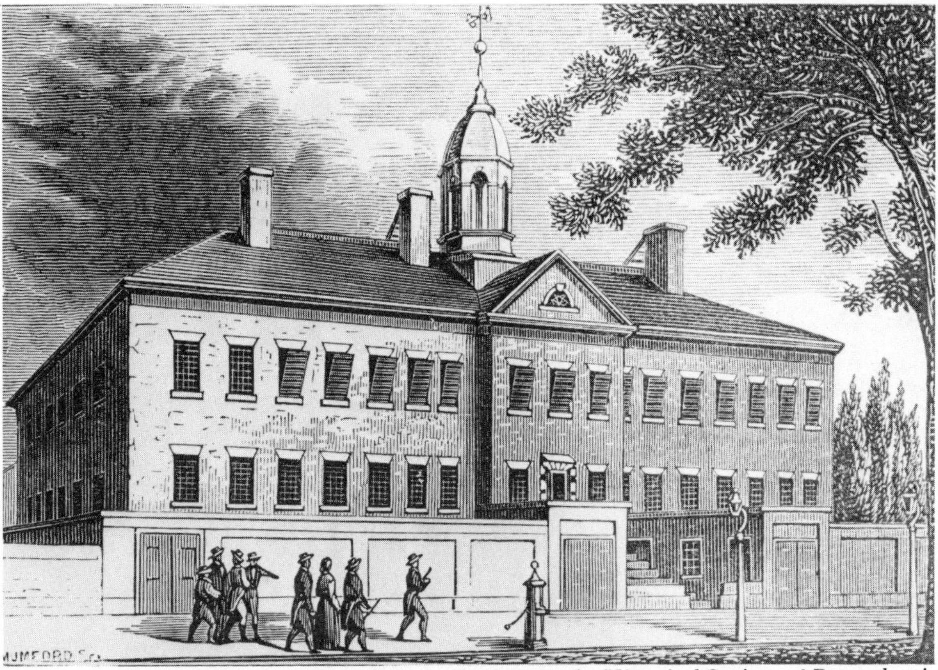

From the collections of the Historical Society of Pennsylvania
The Walnut Street prison, to which the Prune Street jail was an annex.

Morris's unfinished home on Chestnut Street. Engraving of the Poulson sketch.
From the collections of the Historical Society of Pennsylvania

From the collections of the Historical Society of Pennsylvania

Morris's mansion (right) at the corner of Sixth and Market (High) streets, to which he moved after Washington occupied the Morris home at 190 Market (High) Street (also pictured).

sembly, Morris was again officially a public servant, although his public service had scarcely ceased. But occasionally private matters suffered; friends complained of neglect. John Jay, writing from Madrid in November, said:

There are some hearts which like feathers stick to every one they touch, and quit each with equal ease. Mine is not of this kind—it adheres to few, but it takes strong hold. You must therefore write to me, and if you would make your letters very agreeable, dwell on the subjects you will find at or near the Hills and within your own walls. Mrs. Jay writes by this opportunity to Mrs. Morris, whom she loves and esteems for many reasons unnecessary to repeat to you.

Molly was esteemed by many, although often for reasons less heartfelt than Sarah Jay's. A Frenchman who attended a ball given by the French minister, the Chevalier de la Luzerne, "for a select society, on the occasion of a marriage," related that the dancing was interrupted about midnight for a supper. As the guests moved toward the dining room, Luzerne offered his arm to Mrs. Morris and thus gave her precedence over all the other ladies. Such an honor, the visitor noted, was "rather generally bestowed on her, as she is the richest woman in the city, and all ranks here being equal, men follow their natural bent by giving the preference to wealth."

Money had become a crucial concern of Congress. Despite millions of dollars in loans from France and Spain, American finances were tottering. Congress had issued paper money called "Continentals," which dropped so rapidly in value that they were practically worthless.

The mutiny of Pennsylvania troops at Morristown on New Year's Day, 1781, brought the crisis to a head. The soldiers, incensed that each new recruit was being paid a $25 bounty when they themselves had gone unpaid for months, revolted and, under their sergeants, marched toward Philadelphia. Joseph Reed, still president of Pennsylvania's executive council, negotiated with them at Trenton and persuaded them to return to camp, although more than half of them then left the service. Less than three weeks later New Jersey troops mutinied; Washington dispatched soldiers from West Point to subdue the dissidents, and two of the leaders were executed. The mutinies reinforced the increasing calls for financial reform, administrative efficiency, and a strong, centralized government.

Congress therefore decided to abandon its futile attempts to govern solely through its own members, acting as boards and committees, and instead to set up separate departments of finance, war, naval affairs, and foreign affairs. Each department would be headed by an executive responsible to Congress.

The energetic, efficient, acute Robert Morris was the obvious choice for the arduous task of running the department of finance, and on February 20, 1781, he was elected unanimously by Congress, although his enemies Sam Adams and Artemas Ward abstained from the vote.

Gouverneur Morris—a twenty-nine-year-old lawyer and member of Congress from 1777-1779, a dashing young man who had lost a leg as the result of trying to drive a pair of wild horses in a phaeton, one of the aristocratic Morrises of the manor of Morrisania in New York, and no relation to Robert—wrote to the governor of New York, "If he accepts the office which Congress against his will conferred on him, I shall hope to see some better modes of raising money . . . and I shall be morally certain of honesty in the expenditure." Robert was to select Gouverneur as his assistant and make him his friend, a friendship that would last until Robert's death.

Samuel Huntington, then President of Congress, wrote to Robert Morris, "It is hoped that this important call of your country will be received by you, sir, as irresistible." Although Morris wrote Huntington that the contest with Britain had first appeared "just and necessary" and then, as it became dangerous, "I thought it more *glorious*, and was stimulated to the greatest exertions in my power, when the affairs of America were at the worst," he was reluctant to accept the post. If he accepted, certain provisions must be made. He must be permitted to continue his private commercial enterprises. He must have the authority to appoint and dismiss all members of his department, a major consideration in efficient administration.

Even though Congress was reluctant to grant these requests, it gave way, making only minor changes in Morris's stipulation about appointment and dismissal. Finally, on May 14, 1781, Morris, accepting the appointment, pointed out that he was sacrificing "my interest, my ease, my domestic enjoyment and internal tranquillity." But he added that he was so willing to serve his country that he would sacrifice everything save his integrity: "the loss of *that* would effectually disable me from serving . . . more." In his diary he reminded himself that the undertaking was "dangerous" and "contrary to my private interest," that he would be exposed to "the resentment of disappointed and designing men"; however, introducing "system and economy" was essential to "the safety of our country."

From France, Benjamin Franklin sent enthusiastic congratulations, but he warned Morris that:

. . . the public is often niggardly even of its thanks, while you are sure of being censured by malevolent critics and bug-writers, who will abuse you while you are serving them, and wound your character in nameless pamphlets; thereby resembling those dirty little insects, that attack us only in the dark, disturb our repose, molesting and wounding us, while our sweat and blood are contributing to their subsistence. Every assistance that my situation here, as long as it continues, may enable me to afford you, shall certainly be given; for, besides my affection for the glorious cause we are both engaged in, I value myself upon your friendship, and shall be happy if mine can be made of any use to you.

George Washington told Morris, "My hand and heart shall be with you"; to a friend Washington confided that he had great but not unreasonable expectations from Morris's appointment, for he did not suppose that "by Art magick, he can do more than recover us, by degrees, from the labyrinth into which our finance is plunged."

Particularly warm congratulations came from Alexander Hamilton. "I know of no other in America who unites so many advantages," Hamilton said, adding that Morris's efforts would serve to establish American independence: " 'Tis by introducing order into our finances, by restoring public credit, not by winning battles, that we are finally to gain our object."

The sharp-tongued Joseph Reed informed General Nathanael Greene that Morris was "unexorable" and Congress at his "mercy," but that the appointment had vastly simplified Congress's duties: "they are now very much at leisure to read despatches, return thanks, pay and receive compliments, etc." And a Major Armstrong wrote his father that "Bob Morris sets a high price upon his services," and that Congress, in yielding to his demands, had in effect said, " 'I am too great a fool to do my own business.' "

Even before Morris took his oath of office on June 27, 1781, he vigorously began his duties in an office on Front Street near his home; a few months later, when he assumed the additional burden of acting as Agent of Marine, the files and papers were moved to the Marine Office.

Morris's first undertaking was to create a national commercial bank. The Bank of Pennsylvania, having served its purpose, was now inactive. What Morris proposed was an institution to receive deposits, borrow money, print bank notes. By the end of May he had secured official approval from Congress, although the charter was not issued until December 31. The offices were to be located in a remodeled shop on Chestnut Street, not far from Benjamin Franklin's home. To prospective investors Morris said, "We shall only have to appeal to the interest of mankind which in most cases will do more than their Patriotism." But, eager as Morris was to move ahead with the organization of the bank, Washington's urgent needs demanded his immediate energies.

Washington's army desperately needed provisions, especially beef; without supplies, the general said, "our posts cannot be maintained, nor the army be kept in the field much longer."

Morris set out to initiate a drastic innovation. Instead of asking individual states to supply specific items, items whose cost of transportation often exceeded their worth—the method that had unsuccessfully been used to this point—Morris obtained authority from Congress to make contracts with private firms and individuals to supply provisions in exchange for cash. To obtain this cash, Morris resorted to every maneuver he knew; often he drew on his personal credit. Writing to ask Major General Philip Schuyler to deliver a thousand barrels of flour to Washington, Morris pledged that "for your reimbursement you may either take me as a public or private man. . . ." Washington, receiving the flour, acknowledged that "without that aid, we should have been already distressed, and I must candidly confess to you that I see no prospect of being supplied but thro' your means." And two weeks later Washington wrote that "the measures you are pursuing for subsisting the Army perfectly accord with my Ideas, and are, I am certain, the only ones which can secure us from distress or the constant apprehension of it."

France came to Morris's aid in May when the French minister suggested that part of a subsidy be placed at the disposal of the Superintendent of Finance. Morris immediately requested Franklin in Paris to recommend a banker to manage American funds in France. He urged John Jay in Spain to press for funds; his aim, he said, was twofold: "the raising of a revenue with the greatest economy to the public."

In May and early June, Lord Cornwallis, having moved north from the Carolinas, raided deep into Virginia. Opposed by Lafayette, von Steuben, and Anthony Wayne, Cornwallis then moved toward the coast, where he could establish communication by sea with Clinton's forces in New York. Choosing Yorktown, near the lower end of Chesapeake Bay, as his base, he landed there August 1. Meanwhile, Washington learned that his ally, Admiral de Grasse, was sailing from the West Indies with the French fleet, bound for the Chesapeake.

Early in August, Washington asked Morris how many ships

could be obtained at Philadelphia at any time until the twentieth of the month; a new campaign was being planned. Later that week Morris, James Wilson, and Richard Peters, secretary to the Board of War, set out for Washington's headquarters at Dobbs Ferry, New York. They arrived to find Washington out, but on returning at one o'clock to hold his daily levee, he greeted them cheerfully and heartily. At the levee, which lasted more than an hour, were present all the general officers of the American and French troops, the commanders of regiments, heads of departments, and all visitors to camp. The next day, Morris said, he and Peters "had a long conference with the General relative to the numbers of which the army should consist for the next campaign, and the means of reducing the number of officers and augmenting those of privates." When Morris, escorted by an officer and twenty light dragoons, left Dobbs Ferry, he knew that Washington planned to march on Yorktown at once. He also knew that no march would be made if he failed in the monumental feat of supplying transportation and provisions.

On returning to Philadelphia, Morris was worried that news of the campaign was known by too many to maintain secrecy, worried also by the unusually large number of strangers on the streets of the city. Molly and the children were at "The Hills," having taken their beds with them, but Morris, writing to Washington, assured the general that the Morris town house still could provide him with a bed during his stay in Philadelphia and mattresses for his aides.

Morris feverishly made preparations. Beef and pork, both fresh and salted, had to be procured, as well as flour, rum, and tobacco for the men, and hay, Indian corn, and other forage for the horses. Boats and supplies had to be available in Baltimore.

Washington, Rochambeau, and Chastellux reached Philadelphia on August 30, where they were greeted by the First Troop of Philadelphia City Cavalry and escorted to the City Tavern, where the principal citizens had gathered. Then the generals met at Robert Morris's home for dinner.

Troops moved into the city for days—ragged, dirty, tired men. Ships on the Delaware River fired salvos; cheering crowds gathered to welcome the soldiers. When the French arrived, Philadelphians were astonished at how ruddy and handsome the Frenchmen looked. The entire city assumed a more festive air than it had worn for years.

But Morris was too busy for festivities. Each day he conferred with the generals and, between conferences, dashed off letters to governors, businessmen, farmers, soldiers, creditors—letters in which he desperately tried to organize an efficient line of supplies.

Before Washington left Philadelphia on September 5, he had confronted Morris with yet another problem; if Morris failed to solve it, the campaign would halt. The Continental soldiers were threatening not to march much farther if they were not given at least a month's back pay. From Head of Elk (now Elkton), Maryland, Washington wrote despairingly that each day brought increasing necessity for money: ". . . send on a Month's Pay at least, with all the Expedition possible. I wish it to come on the Wings of speed."

Morris dashed around—to Rochambeau, who eventually granted $20,000 of French funds, to friends, to fellow merchants. At last he had the funds Washington requested, most of them obtained by pledging Morris's personal credit. The money was dispatched to Head of Elk with all possible speed, almost on the "Wings" Washington had requested. The troops, satisfied with the token payment, agreed to move on toward Yorktown.

A fleet of about eighty vessels was waiting; by late September the troops, reaching their destination, encamped in a wood about one and a half miles from the village where the British under Cornwallis had fortified themselves. In the meantime, the French fleet under de Grasse had gained command of the sea off Yorktown. By October 19 the British, yielding to the heroic assaults by the Continentals, had capitulated. The redcoats, in splendid new uniforms, marched out to surrender as bands played "The World Turned Upside Down."

An express rider galloped into Philadelphia with news of the victory at three o'clock in the morning of Monday, October 22. Washington's official dispatches appeared two days later and were read to Congress, which, at two o'clock that afternoon, proceeded in a body to the Dutch Lutheran Church to give thanks. On November 3 the British colors taken by Washington arrived. Robert Morris described the event in his diary:

> ... The city troop of light horse went out to meet them, and became the standard bearers, and twentyfour gentlemen, privates in that corps, carried each of them one of the colors displayed. The American and French flags preceding the captured trophies, which were conducted down Market Street to the Coffee House, thence down Front to Chestnut Street, and up that street to the State House, where they were presented to Congress, who were sitting; and many of the members tell me, that instead of viewing their transaction as a mere matter of joyful ceremony, which they expected to do, they instantly felt themselves impressed with the ideas of the most solemn nature. It brought to their minds the distresses our country has been exposed to, the calamities we have repeatedly suffered, the perilous situation, which our affairs have almost always been in; and they could not but recollect the threats of Lord North, that he would bring America to his feet on unconditional terms of submission.

Even though the magnificent victory at Yorktown had effectively crippled British power in America, the redcoats still occupied Savannah, Charleston, Wilmington, and New York City. Peace was on the way, but negotiations moved slowly, and the American soldiers would remain under arms for more than twenty months after the surrender of the British troops at Yorktown.

VI

After Yorktown: Bank Notes and Morris Notes

Soon after the Battle of Yorktown, Robert and Molly Morris made a major decision: to send their two older boys, Robert, Jr., now almost twelve, and ten-year-old Tom, to study abroad. Even though the father had deliberately evaded formal education, he was determined his sons should learn several languages, mathematics, the sciences; "a liberal education," he said, "has its use in every station of life, and I am very anxious that my boys should learn everything that can possibly be useful to them." Not only had American schools been disrupted by the war, but, as Morris told George Washington, "if the example is followed and it becomes the practice to educate American youths in France, habitual attachments will strengthen those ties of affection which in gratitude is due from this to that country." Morris asked Washington to intercede with the Comte de Grasse to obtain passage for the boys on one of the returning French frigates. Travel by sea still was perilous, but the venture was worth the hardships and hazards.

Passage was obtained; from Yorktown on October 27, 1781, Washington sent word that he had just had the pleasure of welcoming the boys to Virginia; "for my Countrys sake, I rejoice in the Sacrifice you are making to your own feelings for the

Education of the young Gentlemen, your Sons. . . ." Washington requested de Grasse to "show them every patronage in your Power to fulfill their Wishes and the Views of their Parents." The boys were accompanied by the Morrises' longtime friend, Matthew Ridley, who married Kitty Livingston, Mrs. John Jay's sister. To Jay, Morris wrote:

> They are tractable, good boys. I hope they will make good men, for that is essential. Perhaps they may become useful to their country, which is very desirable, and if they have genius and judgment, the education they will receive may be the foundation for them to become learned or great men, but this is of the most consequence to themselves.

The boys were tutored in France, then attended school in Geneva, Switzerland. After five years abroad, they spent two additional years at the University of Leipzig. Not long before Robert was to enter the university, his father heard reports that he had become careless about his appearance and clothes. "Whether I am rich or poor can be no reason for your being extravagant or nasty," the elder Morris wrote. He told his teenage son that his ambition was not to give him a large fortune, "but of teaching you how to make one for yourself."

Sending his elder sons off to Europe was a private matter; public concerns soon almost engulfed him. Prior to the victory at Yorktown he had been honored with an exciting but exacting duty, that of Agent of Marine, an appointment confirmed early in September, 1781. As a member of the naval committee, Morris had dealt with naval affairs while Congress was in Baltimore; as an owner of merchant ships and privateers, he had become an efficient and knowledgeable administrator. Morris, burdened as he already was, had hoped that someone else would be selected, or that he would be asked to serve only as a temporary agent. But he undertook the task "because it will at least save money to the public"; he remarked, however, that "true economy, according to my ideas of it, consists in employing a sufficient number of persons to perform the public business."

Morris at once moved the accounts of the Office of Finance to the Marine Office to save time and energy; then he began to do his best to have naval accounts put in order. But interruptions were constant. Even when he had his desk moved to the second floor of the building, creditors with tales of woe pushed past his assistants and clambered up the stairs to confront him.

Even before officially assuming his duties as Agent of Marine, Morris had been attempting to push toward completion the construction of the *America*, a ship of the line under construction at Portsmouth, New Hampshire, since 1777, a vessel that would be the largest in the United States Navy. Morris had been instrumental in having John Paul Jones named her commanding officer, but even the firebrand Jones had encountered obstructions and frustrations in his attempts to get the *America* afloat. Morris, so desperate for money that he had to requisition beef from the chief executive of New Hampshire to feed the workmen, managed to scrape together enough funds to keep construction going.

By September, 1782, the *America* was almost ready for service, to the joy of both Morris and Jones. But then a French ship, the *Magnifique*, was wrecked near Boston Harbor. Morris saw a solution to several dilemmas. Manning and equipping the *America* would place a drain on the Office of Finance that it was not prepared to bear. Moreover, the United States was tremendously in debt to France. Therefore, Morris suggested to Congress that the *America* be given as a gift to France. Congress eagerly accepted the suggestion; the *America*, presented to France, was renamed *Le Franklin*. Jones, hurt and humiliated, protested to Morris that he had not expected, "after having fought and bled for the purpose of contributing to make millions happy and free," that he would "remain miserable and dishonoured by being superseded without any just cause assigned. . . . If I have been instrumental in giving the American Flag some reputation and making it respectable among European Nations, . . . it is not because I have been Honoured by my country with either the proper means or proper encouragment." Although Morris sympathized with Jones's disappointment, he felt that Jones's hopes had to be sacrificed to the more pressing demands of economy and diplomacy.

Meanwhile, Morris pushed ahead with the various elements of his financial policy. As he declared to Franklin in 1782, "There is a period in the progress of things, a crisis between the ardor of enthusiasm and the authority of laws, when much skill and management are necessary to those who are charged with administering the affairs of a nation." His system of supplying the army by contract instead of by requisitions upon the various states already had been inaugurated, as had his plans for a national bank. Wherever possible he introduced measures for cutting expenses by operating the Office of Finance more efficiently; in one day he is said to have dismissed 146 revenue agents and subagents. His long-range purpose was to create public credit, in part by putting pressure upon the states to raise funds by taxation, in part by appealing for foreign loans, in part by continuing to use his own splendid private credit.

In many essential ways, Morris's methods and objectives were similar to the successful policies later inaugurated by Alexander Hamilton; but Morris was ahead of his time, and, more often than not, his exertions proved futile. Perhaps his greatest initial error lay in believing that the states would do their duty when it was pointed out to them; he soon learned that appealing to them was, he said, "like preaching to the dead."

In his letters to the states, which he began circulating early in his administration, Morris implored, beseeched, argued, remonstrated—all to little avail. Most of the states had slight sense of national unity; the governors, eager to maintain their popularity and power at home, did as little as possible to support the central government. At one point Morris confessed failure to Franklin, but confessed with his usual optimism:

The picture I have already given you of this country will not be pleasing to you. Truth bids me add, that it will admit of a higher coloring. But what else could be expected from us? A revolution, a war; the dissolution of government, the creating of it anew; cruelty, rapine, and devastation in the midst of our very bowels. These, Sir, are circumstances by no means favorable to finance. The wonder, then is, that we have done so much, that we have borne so much, and the candid world will add, that we have dared so much.

Morris, as Superintendent of Finance, met the sieges of the new nation's creditors as best he could. He told them that he would pay them with as much delight as they would receive payment, but that he could do nothing until the states levied taxes and the citizens met the levies. To a friend Morris expressed his unhappiness over the impatience of many of the creditors; they would do better, he said, to pay their own taxes and influence their neighbors to pay, "but, whilst the people are grasping at every farthing the public possesses, and no measures are taken to replenish the fountain from whence payments spring, what can they expect?"

Still another source of anguish for Morris was his one-time friend, Silas Deane. In May, 1781, Deane had written to friends in the States that the war was all but lost and urged them to move for a reconciliation; apparently he had arranged with the British to intercept the letters, which were then published as propaganda.

Early in November, Tom Paine requested an interview with Morris about the letters, which had appeared in the New York papers. "I hope this man's knack of creating confusion and involving characters in suspicion is at an end," Paine said. "Whether the letters be genuine or not I do not undertake to give judgement upon, but his language in France is equally as strange as anything contained in these publications."

Morris granted the interview. According to Paine, he admitted that "he had been totally deceived in Deane, but that he now looked upon him to be a bad man, and his reputation totally ruined." Gouverneur Morris also was present, hopping around on his one leg and swearing that "they had all been duped, himself among the rest." Paine said that Gouverneur complimented him "on my quick sight, and, by Gods, says he, nothing carries a man through the world like honesty."

Later, Franklin reported to Robert that Deane "has lost himself entirely, and he and his letters are universally condemned. He can not well return hither [France], and I think hardly to America. I see no place for him but England. He continues, however, to sit croaking at Ghent, chagrined, discontented, and disspirited." Deane sought haven in England; there he was subjected to much the same scorn that greeted Benedict Arnold.

Though Morris's friendship with Deane had proved a bitter disappointment, his friendship with Washington grew increasingly closer. After the victory at Yorktown, Washington began moving his forces northward for an attack on the troops of General Clinton in New York City. On November 26, 1781, the general and Mrs. Washington arrived in Philadelphia and immediately accepted an invitation to the Morrises' town house. That evening Morris, Washington, and Lafayette conferred about additional ways of raising money.

Because Washington had to wait for spring weather to continue his campaign, he decided to spend the winter in Philadelphia. Every Monday evening he conferred with Morris at the Office of Finance. On Christmas Day the Washingtons dined with the Morrises; in accepting the invitation the general said that he was always happy to see Morris, but wished it "to be in your moments of leizure, if any such you have."

Moments of leisure were few, for Morris was pushing ahead with plans for the Bank of North America. On November 1, 1781, he called a meeting of stockholders at the City Tavern. A combination gift and loan from France had enabled Morris to invest $253,000 on behalf of the government in bank shares, a move that brought the bank's subscribed capital to about $325,-000, nearly $75,000 less than Morris had hoped to start with. At the meeting Thomas Willing was elected president of the bank; James Wilson and William Bingham were among the twelve directors. Morris, although he invested private as well as public funds in the bank, never held any office in the organization.

Congress having approved the bank's charter on New Year's Eve, 1781, remodeling of the offices on Chestnut Street near Third was rushed to completion, and the bank opened its doors to the public on January 7, 1782. As Thomas Willing would observe, "The business . . . was a pathless wilderness, ground but little known this side of the Atlantic. . . . Established as merchants, we resolved to pursue the road we were best acquainted with. We established our books on a simple mercantile plan."

The bank issued its own paper money to enable, Morris said, "the individuals of all States a medium for their intercourse with each other and for the payment of taxes more convenient than the precious metals and equally safe." The bank's problem was that the gold and silver in its vaults were much in demand, and the supply dwindled rapidly. According to some stories, when silver was borrowed, secret agents of the bank went after it to persuade the withdrawers to redeposit it. According to other stories, Willing, to make the amount of silver on hand seem impressive, arranged some coins on a circular belt running to the vaults, a belt that showed depositors a seemingly endless display; a porter carried around boxes that were ostentatiously labeled "Silver." Despite these and other devices, the bank at first had difficulty in keeping its bank notes circulating at face value.

The bank's usefulness to the United States was immediately evident. Within six months Morris, as Superintendent of Finance, had borrowed $400,000. The new bank facilitated the superintendent's financial operations and obviously stimulated the economy. Morris soon could declare that the bank had saved America "from the efforts of her avowed and from the intrigues of her concealed enemies," that it had saved her "from those who, while they clamor loudly against the administration for doing so little, sedulously labor to deprive it of the means of doing anything." He claimed that the bank would "exist in spite of calumny, operate in spite of opposition, and do good in spite of malevolence."

By the fall of 1781, Morris had begun circulating paper money that was different from the notes issued by the bank. These pieces of paper, known as "Morris notes," were numbered and signed by Morris, payable "to the Bearer," and could be cashed at the Office of Finance. Morris hoped that these notes, together with the bank notes, would function as a medium of exchange and make collection of taxes easier because they could be used in place of scarce gold and silver. Although the Morris notes were considerably more stable than the Continental currency formerly issued by Congress, they did not completely fulfill the hopes of their originator.

Still another project which Morris urged forward at this time was the establishment of a mint. The two Morrises, Robert and Gouverneur, recognized that American coinage was needed. Using foreign coins as a basis for establishing value was risky, and increasingly coins were coming to have different values in different states. On January 15, 1782, Morris prepared for Congress a report in which he urged that establishing a mint would help to restore public credit:

... although it is possible that the new money will at first be received with diffidence by some, yet when it has been fairly assayed it will gain full confidence from all, and the advantage of holding the only money which can pay debts or discharge taxes will soon give it the preference over all, and indeed banish all other from circulation.

Although Congress approved the proposal, it aroused little interest among the delegates; neither the funds nor the energies were available to bring the project fully to fruition. The United States mint at Philadelphia was not established until 1792.

During all these months Morris was pressing the states to help support the national government. When Congress authorized him to appoint agents in each state to receive the taxes collected for the central government, he made the selections carefully. Whereever possible, he chose men he knew personally, or he asked friends to make recommendations. Agents were to be given a percentage of the monies they collected; the more they succeeded in collecting, the more payment they received.

To twenty-six-year-old Alexander Hamilton, formerly Washington's aide-de-camp and veteran of the battle of Yorktown, Morris offered the post of Receiver of Continental Taxes for the state of New York. Only when assured that the duties would not hinder his study of the law did Hamilton accept. He quickly discovered what Morris already knew: the states enjoyed independence so much that taxation to support a central government seemed unnecessary. "I found every man convinced that something was wrong," he told Morris, "but few that were willing to recognize the mischief when defined and content to the proper remedy." Hamilton threw himself energetically into his duties; he attempted to revamp the fiscal tax system of New York and organize the state's finances. Even so, New York was among the most delinquent states in paying taxes.

From the South, General Nathanael Greene wrote Morris questioning whether taxes could be levied in a region devastated by war, a region where civil government had scarcely been reestablished. Yet he pledged his support, for he realized that, without funds to support the new nation, the war might have been fought in vain.

Early in February, 1782, Morris began warning Congress not to expect many states to meet the quarterly installment of taxes due April 1. In mid-February he circulated a letter to the states exhorting them to levy taxes to meet their quotas. On the first of June, Morris reported to Washington that he had received less than $20,000 of the eight million due in 1782; ironically, the cost of running the war was about $20,000 a day. By the end of July only $50,000 had been collected; on September 1 the total had reached a disappointing $125,000.

Morris's letter to the governor of Connecticut is typical. "That times are hard, that money is scarce, that taxes are heavy and the like, are constant themes of declamation in all countries, and will be so," he said. But, he argued, "men will always find use for all the money they can get hold of and more." And he added, "Hundreds who cannot find money to pay taxes can find it to purchase useless gewgaws and expend much more in the gratification of vanity, luxury, drunkenness, and debauchery, than is necessary to establish the freedom of their country."

In addition to warning Congress that little was to be expected from the states in the way of taxes, Morris pointed out that the men "who trusted us in the hour of distress are defrauded" because their loans were not being repaid; therefore, no citizen would be foolish enough to lend the government more money. And, Morris added, "to expect that foreigners will trust a government which has no credit with its own citizens would be madness." Indeed, even France had said that no further financial aid would be extended. "Our reliance then must be upon ourselves." But the Articles of Confederation, having granted Congress "the privilege of asking everything," had also allowed each state "the prerogative of granting nothing." All Europe stared astonished "at the unparalleled boldness and vastness of claims blended with an unparalleled indolence and imbecility of conduct."

A year earlier Congress had proposed that an import duty be levied "upon all goods, wares, and merchandise of foreign growth and manufacture." Morris had continued to urge that the states adopt such a duty. Now he advised Congress to suggest that states adopt a uniform plan of taxation, including a land tax of a dollar for every hundred acres of land, a poll tax of a dollar on all freemen and all male slaves between sixteen and sixty, and a small excise tax on liquor. Arthur Lee, now in Congress, was on the committee that reported unfavorably on the proposal.

Morris was undaunted. In July, 1782, he sent Congress his Financier's Report on Public Credit, in which he suggested, among other proposals, that import duties must be levied; his recommendations were defeated when voted upon by Congress.

Despite defeats by those more concerned with the welfare of the individual states than with the health of the nation, Morris obstinately maintained his faith in the new country. On the Fourth of July, 1782, he shut the Marine Office and the Office of Finance and sent the clerks home, "that they might be at leisure to indulge those pleasing reflections which every true American must feel on the recollection that six years now are completed since that decisive step taken in favor of the freedom of their country." He also wanted them to "partake of the festivity usual on holidays." Robert and Gouverneur also participated in festivities; the President of Congress "provided a cold collation," and afterward the two Morrises "finished the day with great satisfaction in a select company at the house of a friend."

For most Philadelphians the spring and summer of 1782 were the happiest in many years. In April, Benjamin Franklin began preliminary peace talks in Paris with British representatives, to be joined in June by John Jay and in October by John Adams. Clinton was replaced in New York by Sir Guy Carleton as British commander, and Savannah was evacuated. One of the most splendid parties that Philadelphia had ever seen was given by the Chevalier de la Luzerne in April in honor of the birth of a French Dauphin. More than eleven hundred guests attended, listened to a concert, watched fireworks, ate supper at midnight, and danced until three o'clock in the morning.

The summer brought the Superintendent of Finance some cheering news. Franklin sent word that the French court would loan the United States six million French livres, but warned that the money already was committed to pay European creditors for supplies furnished to America. In August, Franklin informed Morris that his "conduct, activity, and address as a financier and provider for the exigencies of the State, are much admired. . . ."

Aid and hope also came from Holland, where John Adams procured a loan of about $2,000,000 from private firms. Almost inevitably the loan, like others, was largely spent before it actually was received.

Although peace was being negotiated, the Continental army still had to be fed and paid. In October, Morris wrote to Washington, "My Credit has already been in the Brink of Ruin. If that goes, all is gone, but if it can be preserved there will in the last Necessity be some Chance of making advances on Credit to the Army as well as to others." Then he added that "if the States cannot be prevailed on to make greater Exertions it is difficult to foresee where the Thing is to terminate."

By now Morris probably had more enemies than any other public figure—unpaid soldiers, who blamed him for failing to keep promises others had made; angry creditors, who nevertheless failed to pay their taxes; and, above all, those hostile to central control of finances and to Morris as the one man exercising that control. He was continually being sniped at by men such as Joseph Reed, who wrote to General Greene:

Those who know him will also acknowledge that he is too much a man of the world to overlook certain private interests which his command of the paper and occasional speculations in that currency will enable him to promote.... [It has] ever been a ruling principle with him to connect the public service with the private interest.

But Greene heard from Washington that, although Morris was attacked for not having done enough, the public soon would "wonder how Mr. Morris has done so much with so small means."

Morris, defending himself against the charge that his annual salary of $6,000 was excessive, informed Thomas Jefferson that the salary scarcely exceeded the expenses; "a certain degree of splendor is necessary to those who are clothed with the highest offices of the United States.... I speak for my successor, or rather for my country. Neither the powers nor the emoluments of the office have sufficient charms to keep me in it one hour after I can quit it."

To protect himself and his office from charges of wrongdoing, he had told James Madison of Virginia, a man described by a contemporary as "no bigger than half a piece of soap," that he wanted to have Congressional committees examine his books twice yearly, "from a conviction that the more they know of my proceedings the more they will be convinced of my constant desire and exertions to promote the honor and the interest of the United States." Madison later wrote to a friend in Virginia that he could not excuse the malice with which Morris's character was being murdered:

> I have seen no proof of misfeasance. I have heard many charges which were palpably erroneous. I have known others, somewhat suspicious, vanish on examination. Every member in Congress must be sensible of the benefit which has accrued to the public from his administration; no intelligent man out of Congress can be altogether insensible of it.

The charges, voiced by Joseph Reed, that Morris had profited privately from his public position were whispered about everywhere. A visitor, the Prince de Broglie, set down in his diary a characterization reflecting both the praise and the blame he had heard:

> Mr. Morris is a large man, who has a reputation for honourableness and intelligence. It is certain that he has great credit at least; and that he has been clever enough, while appearing often to make advances of his own funds for the service of the republic, to accumulate a great fortune and to gain several millions since the Revolution began.

The prince had been taken by the French minister, the Chevalier de la Luzerne, to have tea with the Morrises. De Broglie noted that Mrs. Morris was dressed largely in white and that the house was "simple, but neat and proper," that the doors and tables were of "superb mahogany, carefully treated," and that the copper locks and trimmings were "charmingly neat."

The tea de Broglie received was "excellent," he said. Indeed, he had just finished his twelfth cup when Luzerne told him to put his spoon across the cup when he wanted "this species of torture by hot water to stop." Luzerne explained that "it is almost as bad manners to refuse a cup of tea when it is offered to you as it would be indiscreet for the master of the house to offer you some more, when the ceremony of the spoon has shown what your intentions are in respect to this matter."

Luzerne frequently visited the Morris home. On October 3,

1782, he lent distinction to an already distinguished company—congressmen, the Spanish resident in Philadelphia, the heads of various departments—who had assembled at a dinner in honor of the acknowledgment of American independence by Holland. The evening, Morris observed, was spent in "great festivity, suitable toasts being drank for the occasion."

Despite defeats by Congress, despite attacks by malevolent enemies, despite sieges by the nation's creditors, Morris remained faithful. As he commented to Alexander Hamilton: "A firm, wise, manly System of federal Government is what I once wished, what I now Hope, what dare not expect, but what I will not despair of."

VII

Efforts to "Keep the Money-Machine a Going"

January, 1783, opened with a crisis for Morris and for Congress. Late in December a group of officers headed by General Alexander McDougall came to Philadelphia to demand back pay from Congress, especially half-pay that had been promised in 1778 and again in 1780. They said that they had "borne all that men can bear—our property is expended—our private resources are at an end, and our friends are wearied out and disgusted with our incessant applications." With the war seemingly over, the officers feared that some would argue that promises made in the heat of war need not be honored, and such arguments indeed were being heard.

The two Morrises in the Office of Finance knew that immediate payment was impossible because funds were lacking. Deciding to treat the army as yet another category of public creditors, Robert and Gouverneur seized the opportunity to press Congress and the states to adopt a program to fund the debts of the Confederation. A committee of Congress called on Robert, who disclosed that the government already had overdrawn its accounts in Europe; Congress granted approval to overdraw the accounts even more. The Morrises then told McDougall that the army would receive a month's pay at the rate of about half a dollar a week. Soldiers and noncommissioned officers were to receive cash; officers would get notes payable in sixty days.

While this crisis was reaching its climax in Philadelphia, in the South General Nathanael Greene heard disturbing rumors, rumors that led him to voice the fear that Robert Morris was about to resign.

Morris himself had become convinced that resignation was necessary. In part, he believed that, because so much of the public credit rested on his private credit, his resignation would force Congress and the states to take positive steps toward adopting the financial program he had proposed.

On January 24, 1783, he submitted a letter of resignation to the President of Congress. Only public danger had persuaded him to accept the post, he said, a task that he had continued to labor at despite great difficulties and little support. Now the danger from war was past. "But now," he stated, "other circumstances have postponed the establishment of public credit in such a manner that I fear it will never be made. To increase our debts, while the prospect of paying them diminishes, does not consist with my idea of integrity." Therefore, he said, he had to quit a situation which had become "utterly insupportable."

So that public matters would not "be deranged by any precipitation," Morris was willing to continue serving until May 1, but if effectual measures were not taken by that time to provide permanently for public debts of every kind, Congress would have to appoint a new Superintendent of Finance. "I should be unworthy of the confidence reposed in me by my fellow-citizens if I did not explicitly declare, that I will never be the minister of injustice."

This letter, James Madison reported, made "a deep and solemn" impression on Congress. Obviously Morris was despondent about "seeing justice done to the public creditors, or the public finances placed on an honourable establishment." Morris's resignation would create dangers. When known, it would provide fresh hope to the enemy, it would ruin both domestic and foreign economy, and it would produce, Madison asserted, "a vacancy which none knew how to fill, and which no fit man would venture to accept."

Not all would view Morris's action as generously as Madison did. Some would suggest that Morris was impatient, petulant, that he lacked fortitude amid neglect and inefficiency.

Imposing secrecy on the contents of Morris's letter, Congress began investigating ways to fund the public debt. Both Alexander Hamilton and Gouverneur Morris urged Washington and other key army officers to exert pressure upon Congress; this activity soon gave rise to accusations that Robert Morris had prompted civil commotions. The debate in Congress clearly revealed that almost all members wished to find a way of satisfying the creditors, but those who supported a strong union suggested one way, and those who wished to see strong states and a weaker union suggested other ways.

In February, at Morris's insistence, Congress lifted the ban of secrecy on the resignation. Washington, regarding the consequences as unfortunate, even fearful, urged Morris to continue despite the embarrassments. Morris expressed hope to Nathanael Greene that the general would understand why he felt impelled to leave a post "where I must be daily the witness to scenes of poignant anguish and deep injustice without the possibility of administering either relief or palliation." But at much the same time Joseph Reed communicated to Greene his sentiments that Morris had long been a figure "whose dictates none dare oppose, and from whose decisions lay no appeal; he has, in fact, exercised the power really of three great departments, and Congress have only had to give their fiat to his mandates."

In the *Freeman's Journal* a writer signing himself "Lucius" launched a vitriolic attack on Morris, an attack which the Superintendent protested was "replete with the most infamous falsehoods and assertions without the least shadow of truth to support them and insinuations as base and infamous as envy and malignancy could suggest."

"Lucius" accused Morris of wishing to make his will law, of acquiring great wealth from speculation amid the distresses of war, of having become inebriated with his own pride, of dishonesty and false patriotism:

You produce yourself as the Atlas on which the United States entirely rest—Your time, property, and domestic bliss are sacrificed to the salvation of the public. Is, then, the mere superintendence of our finances with an assistant and a legion of clerks, at ten paces from your family, so mighty a sacrifice of time—is daily rioting in Asiatic luxury at festive boards so fatal to domestic bliss— . . . is the full enjoyment of your mercantile connections with the immense advantages over all other merchants which your office gives to you and your partners, such puny emoluments as to render the possession of them so glaring a sacrifice of your property?

. . . In fine, Sir, is not the disbursement of eight millions annually in contracts, etc., is not the profit and influence arising from this; is not the hourly offering of incense and adulation from surrounding parasites; is not the pushing of your superlative abilities and merits by pensioned dependents throughout all the states, sufficient to satiate your vanity, pride, and avarice? . . .

Numbers are serving their country in the cabinet and in the field, remote from their country, their family, and their affairs, without patronage, without emolument, without influence, upon pay which would hardly purchase the crumbs which fall from your luxurious table, and yet we do not hear from them, the vainglorious whinings of their sacrifices and sufferings.

Biased and filled with invective though this attack was, it accurately reflected the attitude of many toward Morris. He possessed wealth, power, influence; his home was elegant. To the unpaid, poorly fed soldiers, to the creditors threatened with debtors' prison because the United States had not repaid their loans, Morris, as the paymaster who refused to pay, seemed a diabolical monster.

Meanwhile, progress had been made toward peace with Britain. On April 15, 1783, Congress ratified the provisional treaty of peace, but censured the American commissioners for having proceeded without properly consulting the French. The final treaty was ratified almost nine months later.

Early in April, Hamilton, on behalf of Congress, approached Morris about a plan for establishing a peacetime navy. Although Morris volunteered to assist the project, he suggested that, because he was planning to leave public office, Congress would be wiser to appoint a Minister of Marine, "who might now form the Plans he is to execute."

Soon after this conference Hamilton wrote to Washington to justify Morris's conduct and to emphasize how backward Congress had been in pushing for funds. With the states failing to provide taxes, with new European loans in doubt, with the army pressing for supplies, Morris had been reduced to the alternative "either of making engagements which he could not fulfill or declaring his resignation in case funds were not established by a given time." Hamilton pointed out that if Morris had followed the first course, "the bubble must soon have burst," and his private character and credit, as well as public credit, would have been ruined. Morris hoped, Hamilton said, that the threat of resignation would stimulate Congress to action. But Hamilton confessed that he thought Morris was "ill-advised" and "imprudent" to have published his letter of resignation. Yet no man but he "could have kept the money-machine a going during the period he has been in office. From every thing that appears, his administration has been upright as well as able."

The debate over Morris's resignation continued to rage in Congress. Hamilton, Madison, and three other members were appointed a committee to negotiate with Morris to determine on what terms he might be persuaded to continue; after meeting with the committee Morris recorded in his diary, ". . . if they think my Assistance essential I will Consent to remain in Office for the Purpose of Compleating such Payment to the Army as may be agreed. . . ."

Fears increased that the army would mutiny if not paid. The measures finally proposed in Congress fell far short of what Morris, Hamilton, and others had hoped for. Congress recommended that the states adopt a duty on all imports, that each state be assigned a quota of a $1,500,000 requisition, and that the cession of western lands be hastened. Morris saw these measures as a defeat of his program, and, although no one can be certain that his program would have worked, it might have produced more prosperity than the effects Congress's program created.

On May 3 Morris agreed to continue temporarily in office, although ten days earlier he had noted in his diary, "I wish for nothing so much as to be relieved from this cursed Scene of Drudgery and Vexation."

Morris at once began trying to marshal funds to pay the army. He estimated that $750,000 in hard money would be needed for three-months' pay, money that should come from taxes and the sale of public lands in the West. However, because the states were not exerting themselves, an issue of paper money in anticipation of taxes seemed a necessity, an act which, Morris said, would render him liable "personally for about half a Million when I leave this Office." Beseeching both Luzerne and Franklin for aid in obtaining the funds, he confided to the latter, "Nothing should induce me in my private character to make such applications for money as I am obliged to do in my public character." Although arrangements might have been made with the Bank of North America for an issue of paper money, Morris decided to rely instead upon his "Morris notes," to be due in six months.

By the end of the second week in June, Morris had signed about six thousand notes worth more than $200,000; the notes were to be redeemed by the receivers of Continental taxes in the states. Disastrously, by the time the notes reached the camp at Newburgh, New York, many of the men already had departed on furloughs authorized by Congress to last until their official discharge. Soldiers in some regions of the nation, when the notes reached them, were forced to sell them at a fraction of their value to feed themselves and their families. In other regions the notes seem to have maintained almost their face value. As Morris revealed to Jay, "The army was dispersed, and since their departure the men who urged these measures most, and who are eternally at war with honor and integrity, have been continually employed in devising measures to prevent my being able to fulfill my engagements, in hopes of effecting my ruin in case of failure."

All Philadelphia was soon to be upset by the army's dissatisfaction. On June 17 about eighty Continental soldiers began a march from Lancaster under arms and under their sergeants to collect their back pay. Hearing of the soldiers' approach, Morris first sent for Thomas Willing, president of the bank, to advise him to take protective measures. Next he rushed home to tell Molly and the children not to be alarmed if the soldiers approached the house. Then, to lessen the danger to his family, he decided to leave his own house and take refuge in a friend's house, where the soldiers would not be likely to find him.

By noon on Saturday, June 21, the men from Lancaster had been joined by several hundred additional soldiers from regiments in Philadelphia. The President of Congress, Elias Boudinot, hastily called a session of the members in the State House, where the executive council of Pennsylvania under its president, John Dickinson, also was meeting. No sooner had the two groups assembled than the mutineers, with fixed bayonets, surrounded the State House.

The soldiers waited outside; the beseiged legislators waited within. Soon the mutineers sent in a document which, in its vigorous language, was obviously not a humble petition, a document setting forth their grievances. Congress and the executive council at once became embroiled in an argument over which group should do what. Finally, the members of Congress resolved to sit quietly until three o'clock, the customary hour for adjournment. Outside, the soldiers lounged, using violent language but refraining from violent acts, although a few occasionally "wantonly pointed their Muskets to the Windows of the Hall of Congress." At three o'clock the congressmen nervously arose, sauntered with as much jauntiness as they could muster to the door, and proceeded out of the building through the ranks of their captors. The soldiers offered only "a mock obstruction"; then, with their captives at large, the men returned to their barracks. Robert Morris, a few blocks away, had gone undetected and unscathed.

Increasingly, rumors circulated that the soldiers were planning vehement—perhaps violent—action. On Tuesday, June 24, President Boudinot proclaimed that Congress should adjourn to Princeton and reassemble there two days later "in order that further and more effectual measures may be taken for suppressing the present revolt, and maintaining the dignity and authority of the United States." Hamilton, in particular, had urged flight; he feared that the Superintendent of Finance or some of the congressmen might be seized as hostages.

Congress fled, and so did Robert and Gouverneur Morris. Robert ordered that business at the Office of Finance should be suspended. Leaving the secretary as caretaker of the building and papers, the Superintendent told him that, "in case the soldiers came with mischievous intent, to inform them that the whole army are interested in those papers, and indeed all America, and that they must expect the resentment of the whole if any destruction is committed."

Once Congress had left, the mutiny rapidly disintegrated. The soldiers, repenting, laid down their arms and accused their sergeants of having betrayed and misled them. Some of the men from Lancaster attempted to hold out, but gave way before the threats of their comrades.

The two Morrises were forced to remain at Trenton and Princeton for more than a week. Boudinot feared that harm might come to them in Philadelphia, but at last gave them permission to return to their duties. Robert seems to have recovered quickly from whatever distress he felt over the uproar, for on the Fourth of July he noted in his diary, "Finding on my return that no public entertainment was provided for this day, I invited a company of forty gentlemen consisting of foreigners, military and civil officers, and citizens, and spent the afternoon and evening in great festivity and mirth."

Throughout the fall of 1783, Morris struggled valiantly to stave off a collapse of credit. Congress and the states did little to help; his problems were increased by the fact that attempts to float a loan in Holland were hampered by news of the mutiny in June. Morris's enemies continued their malevolent attacks. James Warren, for example, wrote to John Adams, "Morris is a King, and more than a King. He has the Keys of the Treasury at his Command, Appropriates Money as he pleases, and every Body must look up to him for Justice and for Favour." And William Lee recorded his opinion: "Morris seems to be the most dangerous man in America, from the particular attention that is paid to every creature, dependent, and connection of his that appears in Europe, by Franklin and John Adams,—two men that are rivals in all the low cunning and tricks of politics."

By the fall Morris was making active attempts to revive his private interests, which had been largely neglected during his years as Superintendent of Finance. The most important of these ventures he revealed in a letter to Jay on November 27, "I am sending some ships to China, in order to encourage others in the advantageous pursuits of commerce. . . ." The *Empress of China*, owned equally by Daniel Parker and Company and Robert Morris, sailed for Canton in January, 1784. She carried a cargo of ginseng, brandy, wine, tar, and turpentine—and she was well-armed with guns in case of attack. The voyage of the *Empress* was successful; "she has opened new objects to all America," Morris joyfully remarked.

Late in 1784, Washington attempted to place his nephew in a position in Morris's countinghouse. None was available, Washington reluctantly informed his brother, but added that such a position would have had considerable advantages "because his Mercantile knowledge and connections, greatly exceed that of any other person's upon this Continent and are perhaps equal to what can be found in any other quarter."

During most of 1784, Morris abandoned his efforts to suggest long-range financial policies to Congress and the states; instead, he concentrated his energies on meeting obligations that were due and seeing that administrative affairs ran as smoothly as possible. Occasionally the impudence of creditors provoked him, as is evident in his response to four army officers: "Gentlemen: I have received, this morning, your application. I make the earliest answer to it. You demand instant payment. I have no money to pay you with. Your most obedient and humble servant, Robert Morris."

Month by month during 1784 Morris succeeded in reducing the amounts outstanding for the "Morris notes," and by the time he returned to private life on November 1 he had discharged the debt incurred in meeting the army's claims and had balanced his budget. The battle had been conducted without fanfare, but, to Morris at least, it was one of the most glorious of the victories leading to the creation of a new nation.

His outspoken belief in a strong central government had made him many foes. But, as he said, "The inhabitants of a little hamlet may feel pride in a sense of separate independence. But if there be not one government which can draw forth and direct the combined efforts of our united America, our independence is but a name, our freedom a shadow, and our dignity a dream."

VIII

Another Ship to China . . . and the Constitutional Convention

The first major struggle in which Robert Morris engaged after leaving office as Superintendent of Finance was the battle to save the Bank of North America, whose charter was repealed by the Pennsylvania Assembly on September 13, 1785. Morris, although not a member of the bank's board of directors, was suspected of largely dominating the bank's policy; his enemies, regarding him as aristocratic, wealthy, powerful, sought to diminish his supposed power whenever they could.

The Bank of North America increasingly was viewed as a threat to democracy by its opponents. By absorbing a proposed rival bank, it came to be regarded as a monopoly that eventually might restrain trade. Because it paid its shareholders dividends reportedly as high as 16 per cent, it was accused of charging excessive interest on its loans, of preying on those who borrowed from it. Perhaps the most effective propaganda against the bank was that it was capitalistic, an organization that, by allowing a handful of men to control the wealth of the country, would ultimately enable those few to control the government.

When the Assembly revoked the charter, the bank became the major issue in the next Pennsylvania election. Robert Morris, after a vigorous campaign, won a seat in the Assembly and immediately took the lead in the fight to restore the charter. In a heated debate he recounted the history of the bank, especially the history of its important aid to the United States when he was Superintendent of Finance. Political maneuvering continued for many months, but the charter was at last restored in 1787.

During this period Morris's business ventures multiplied. From the Farmers-General, a group of French financiers who had a monopoly on importing tobacco into France, Morris and a partner secured an exclusive contract for 60,000 hogsheads of tobacco. His supervision of this facet of his vast mercantile enterprises often took him to Virginia, where Washington, as his diary reveals, took delight in entertaining the Philadelphia merchant at Mount Vernon.

One of Morris's many other ventures involved the *Alliance*, a ship commanded during the war by Captain John Barry, who, in April, 1781, had forced two British men-of-war to surrender. Morris, purchasing the *Alliance*, prepared her for new glory. Refitting her for mercantile service and arming her with two twelve-pounders, he decided to attempt a perilous feat: to dispatch the vessel to China in a season regarded as fraught with danger for shipping. With the aid of Gouverneur, Robert mapped out the route for the captain, Thomas Reed, which called for him to sail around Australia to avoid hostile winds. When the *Alliance*, having weathered all storms during a six-months' voyage, arrived at Canton on December 22, 1787, all those who had expressed skepticism about the venture were astounded. Once again Robert Morris's recklessness had been vindicated.

By now Robert and Molly had moved from their home on Front Street to the already famous house at 190 High (Market) Street. The house, which originally had belonged to the family of Richard Penn's wife, had been occupied by General Howe and then by Benedict Arnold. John Holker, the French consul, was living there in January, 1780, when a fire almost destroyed the residence. Morris, having rebuilt the house, obtained title to it in 1785. It became the scene of constant social activity, a purpose for which it was splendidly suited. On the street floor were the entrance hall, a magnificent staircase, and two dining rooms, one for the family, one for formal dinners, a room for upper servants, and a kitchen. On the floor above were two drawing rooms, bedrooms, and a "bathing room." The third floor and the garret contained additional bedrooms. Among the servants were coachmen, footmen, a butler, a housekeeper, a confectioner, and a French cook. Washington would later complain that the stable had room for only twelve horses.

Everyone knew that Morris had a passion for furnishing the house elegantly, and the passion gave rise to a story that was widely circulated. As a gift to Congress, Louis XVI, King of France, sent portraits of himself and Queen Marie Antoinette, but the French minister, Marbois, was unable to deposit the portraits because Congress as yet had no permanent seat. About to return to France in 1785, Marbois asked Morris to be responsible for the still uncrated portraits until they could be delivered to Congress, but then, hearing that Morris was preparing to unpack the pictures, sent a letter of protest. Morris's reply showed obvious irritation over what he took to be the suggestion that he was, out of vanity, planning to hang the portraits in his own home; he insisted that the art, uncrated, would be easier to store. Marbois' reply, a model of courtesy, repudiated any suspicion of Morris, but—so the story went—suggested that he would find time to present the portraits, whether or not Congress had a permanent home.

Throughout 1785 and 1786, as weaknesses in the Articles of Confederation became increasingly evident, demands for changes gained ground. In the spring of 1785 representatives from Maryland and Virginia, meeting at Mount Vernon to settle a dispute over navigation of the Potomac River, suggested that delegates from all states attend a convention at Annapolis to find ways of removing hindrances to interstate trade. Robert Morris was an obvious choice to be one of Pennsylvania's representatives at the Annapolis Convention in September, 1786. This convention, at which only five states were represented, urged that another convention be called the following May in Philadelphia, to "take into consideration the situation of the United States, to devise such further provisions as shall appear to them necessary to render the Constitution of the Federal Government adequate to the exigencies of the Union." In February, 1787, Congress invited the thirteen states to send delegates for a convention scheduled to start on May 14 for the sole purpose of revising the Articles of Confederation.

By May, Philadelphians could tell that the summer would be one of the hottest in years; the humidity was intense. Robert Morris, elected a delegate from Pennsylvania, must have felt regret at being forced to forego the summer at his beloved—and cool—"The Hills."

George Washington arrived in Philadelphia the day before the convention was to begin—a bright Sunday, made noisy by cheering crowds, chiming bells, booming artillery. A smartly uniformed troop of light horsemen—a vivid contrast to the tattered troops he had commanded—met his carriage at the ferry on the Schuylkill River and escorted him to his intended lodgings at a Mrs. House's, at Fifth and Market streets, where James Madison had taken up quarters ten days earlier. But Robert and Molly Morris, whose gracious home was less than a block away, met Washington when he arrived at Mrs. House's and insisted that he stay with them, a prospect so pleasant that he accepted with alacrity. Washington's first formal act was to journey the few blocks to the home of the aged Benjamin Franklin, like Morris a delegate to the convention from Pennsylvania. There Washington was served with either a cask of porter, according to one story, or a cup of tea, according to another.

The next day, when the delegates met at the State House, only Pennsylvania and Virginia were represented; eleven days would elapse before a quorum of seven states was present. During these early sessions the Virginians drafted the fifteen resolutions that were to become the basis of the new Constitution, resolutions that included proposals for a Congress consisting of a lower house elected by the people and an upper house selected by the lower; Congress would elect national judges and the chief executive.

The meetings of the Federal Convention were held in the same chamber in which the Continental Congress had met. Because of the many wide, lofty windows the large room was not especially gloomy even when heavy rain fell outside, as it did on May 29, when the quorum of twenty-nine delegates presented their credentials and chose a secretary. On behalf of the Pennsylvania delegation, Robert Morris then rose and nominated Washington as president of the convention, a motion seconded by John Rutledge. The vote was unanimous; Morris and Rutledge led Washington to the presiding officer's high-backed chair against the paneled east wall.

The fifty-five delegates who finally enrolled at the convention sat at wide tables, draped with green baize, three or four men at a table. Rarely were all delegates present, but Morris's record for attendance was steady.

The State House was only a block from Morris's home, which became more than ever a center of social and political activity. One evening toward the end of June a large company had assembled there for dinner. A knock was heard at the door, and a man appeared with news that Morris's drafts had been protested as worthless, in London; Washington noted in his diary that the interruption was "a little mal-apropos."

Molly Morris, eager to be hospitable, invited Washington to hear an Irish lady "in reduced circumstances" read and speak on the Powers of Eloquence at College Hall; she also accompanied him to a concert in one of the elegant club rooms at the City Tavern. Washington often distracted his host and hostess by slipping into the house unannounced and unobserved; Molly or Robert would suddenly discover the general working over his papers. Washington observed that Molly was "a notable lady in family arrangements," and eventually he bought her a secondhand mangle for pressing clothes, much like the one he had observed with interest at Benjamin Franklin's.

Whenever the convention enjoyed a recess, Washington and the Morrises made excursions out of the city to escape the stifling heat. They went to Trenton to fish, or they drove out to "The Hills" to enjoy the gardens and orchards. On one occasion they went up the Schuylkill River to "one Jane Moore's," where Washington and Gouverneur Morris, who had joined the expedition, cast for trout in a little creek. Then Washington rode on to inspect the earthworks his troops had erected at Valley Forge years earlier.

Although the delegates were convivial, meeting in the evenings to talk at one or another of Philadelphia's pleasant taverns —the City Tavern, the Indian Queen, the Black Horse, the George—during the days they labored steadily and earnestly at the State House in a sweltering room whose many windows generally were kept closed to prevent eavesdropping by curious outsiders. Debates were spirited and forceful.

At the end of May the Virginia Plan, which suggested far more than merely a revision of the Articles of Confederation and laid the basis for a central government of far-reaching power, was presented. In mid-June the New Jersey Plan, supported by the small states, was offered; it suggested retaining the Confederation but granting Congress powers to tax, to regulate commerce, and to name a plural executive and a Supreme Court; and it called for a Congress of only one house, in which the states would be equally represented. By July the convention seemed to have arrived at a stalemate.

The importance of Morris's contribution to the convention has been questioned. James Madison, who kept careful notes on the proceedings, recorded only one occasion after nominating Washington when Morris addressed the delegates: on June 25 he seconded George Reed's motion that senators of the United

States should continue holding office "during good behavior." Some have found Robert's silence a "pathetic" contrast to the vigorous activity of his friend Gouverneur. Others have argued that he was active behind the scenes, that his advice was heeded with respect by Washington, Hamilton, and the younger Morris, that he was silent publicly but powerful privately. And Morris still had enemies so vindictive that they would have strongly opposed any measure which he outspokenly supported.

William Pierce, a delegate from Georgia, recorded the following observation about Morris during the convention: "He has an understanding equal to any public object and possesses an energy of mind that few men can boast of. Although he is not learned, yet he is as great as those who are."

If Robert Morris was not learned, he was determined that his sons, Robert, Jr., and Thomas, now at the University of Leipzig, should be. While delegates to the convention were meeting, he wrote to the boys,

> You, my children, ought to pray for a successful issue to their labours, as the result is to be a form of government under which you are to live, and in the administration of which you may hereafter probably have a share, provided you qualify yourselves by application to your studies. The laws of nations, a knowledge of the Germanic system and the constitutions of the several governments in Europe, and an intimate acquaintance with ancient and modern history are essentially necessary to entitle you to participate in the honor of serving a free people in the administration of their government.

On Monday, July 16, the delegates felt more refreshed than they had been in weeks. Over the weekend a cooling breeze had come down from the northwest, and Philadelphians slept well. That Monday the convention finally accepted the Great Compromise—the Connecticut Compromise—proposed by Roger Sherman of Connecticut: that representation in the lower house be proportional to population and in the Senate be based on one vote for each state. With this barrier surmounted, a committee proceeded to draft a constitution of twenty-three articles. On

September 16 Gouverneur was asked to prepare the final draft, which he had ready two days later. Thirty-nine of the forty-two delegates present on the day the formal copy was ready signed the document. As Robert Morris placed his signature on the parchment, he became one of two men—Roger Sherman was the other—to have signed three major documents: the Declaration of Independence, the Articles of Confederation, and the Constitution of the United States.

A letter then was prepared transmitting the document to Congress, and the convention adjourned. Most of the members, according to Washington, proceeded to the City Tavern, "dined together, and took a cordial leave of each other." Washington then strolled back to the Morrises', where he retired "to meditate on the momentous work."

IX

Senator Morris . . . and Speculator Morris

When Robert Morris resigned as Superintendent of Finance in 1784, his relentless enemy Arthur Lee was one of a three-man committee appointed to supervise the affairs of the treasury. Lee, pursuing his duty, tried to unravel the accounts of the old Secret Committee; pursuing Morris, he seems to have furnished information to those hostile to Morris and the Federation that Morris supported, men who used the fragmentary information as the basis for venomous attacks starting late in 1787.

At this point a bitter contest was being fought in Pennsylvania over the proposed Federation and the adoption of the Constitution. Late in November the Federalists, who supported the Constitution, most of them from Philadelphia and other commercial centers, managed to win significant victories over the Anti-Federalists; and Pennsylvania ratified the Constitution on December 12. But the bitterness between the two factions did not end with ratification.

In the press one of the leading attackers of Morris was a clever, vitriolic writer who signed himself "Centinel." Describing Morris as "a public defaulter" and "a man without principles," "Centinel" charged that he never had settled his accounts with the government.

At the time that "Centinel's" denunciations appeared, Robert Morris, with his associate, Gouverneur, was in the South, where the two men had journeyed to inspect vast tracts of land for which Robert, now caught up in the fever of land speculations, was negotiating. Virginia had not yet ratified the Constitution; the battle there was as bitter as the one in Pennsylvania, with Patrick Henry leading the offense and James Madison fighting for the defense. Morris realized that his friendship with Washington and visits to Mount Vernon were public knowledge; he feared that "Centinel's" attacks on him were intended largely to discredit the Federalist cause in Virginia. As a result, Morris, violating his own rule against debating in the public press, dispatched a letter from Richmond to Philadelphia's *Independent Gazetteer*, where it was published on April 8, 1788. Morris reproached himself in a diary entry: "A newspaper is certainly an improper place for starting and settling public accounts, especially those which are already before the popular tribunal."

In the letter Morris stated that in the early days of the Revolution he had been authorized to import and export and to deposit American funds in Europe. "To effect these objects I received considerable sums of money," Morris said; "the business has been performed, but the accounts are not yet settled." The settlement had been delayed because Morris had not yet been able to obtain receipts for some deliveries and duplicates of accounts lost at sea during the war, but he had not rushed because he believed the balance to show him to be the government's creditor rather than its debtor. As for his transactions as Superintendent of Finance, he said that no accounts required settlement. "As I never received any of the public money none of it can be in my hands," he asserted. All money was received by or paid from the public treasury on Morris's warrants. "The party to whom it was paid was accountable; and the accounts were all in the treasury office, open (during my administration) to the inspection of every American citizen." Morris claimed that only "the propriety of the issue to others by my authority" was his responsibility; all government receipts had regularly been published in the papers, and all his transactions had been under the surveillance of Congress.

For the moment the battle ceased, but Morris's enemies had not yet settled their accounts with him.

Despite these attacks, the spring of 1788 was joyous, for his sons, Robert, Jr., and Thomas, returned after a seven years' absence in Europe. Robert soon was placed in charge of the Morris affairs at Morrisville, Pennsylvania, land that Morris had purchased near the Falls of Trenton. Thomas was to supervise operations on still other Morris holdings, a tract in western New York State. In May, Washington, writing to Molly, congratulated her on the "happy event" of her sons' return and expressed his delight that Robert, Molly, Maria, and the two young men were about to visit Mount Vernon. He suggested that she bring the other children—William, Hetty, Charles, and three-year-old Henry, who had been born on July 24, 1784; "with much truth we can assure you of the pleasure it would give us to see them all under this roof with you and Mr. Morris."

The year 1788 also brought a departure. Just before Christmas, Gouverneur Morris sailed for France, where he would remain until 1798. In large part he was going on business for Robert: to straighten out certain tangles in the tobacco contract with the Farmers-General, to sell the lands Robert had purchased in western New York, to purchase cargoes for resale by Robert to the French West Indies. Among his public duties he was to attempt to persuade private French bankers to help fund the American debt to France.

The battle over ratification of the Constitution had been won by June 21, when the ninth state, New Hampshire, acted. By the end of July, Virginia and New York also had ratified; in North Carolina ratification was carried on November 21. Rhode Island delayed ratification until May, 1790. In September, 1788, Congress set New York City as the temporary site of the new government and the following March as the date of the first meeting of a Congress under the new Constitution.

Ratification of the Constitution brought Robert Morris to a new phase in his career. The Pennsylvania Assembly selected him as one of the first two United States senators from Pennsylvania, his term to run from 1789 to 1795. His colleague was to be a stout, muscular, sharply opinionated man—at six feet, three inches, even taller than Morris—William Maclay of Maclayville, later Harrisburg.

Senator Robert Morris arrived at the temporary capital at New York City at seven o'clock in the morning of March 4, 1789, so early that his host, William Constable, a New York merchant and banker with whom Morris had business dealings, had not yet arisen. That evening Morris wrote to Molly that, when Congress assembled in the morning, only eight senators and thirteen representatives were present, not enough for a quorum; twelve senators and thirty representatives were needed. He reported that the previous night at the Battery thirteen cannon had been fired over the funeral of the Confederation, and that this morning eleven cannon were fired, one for every state except North Carolina and Rhode Island, who had not yet ratified the Constitution. The ringing of bells and the cheering of crowds had given the opening of Congress "the air of a grand Festival."

Not until April 6 did the twelfth senator, Richard Henry Lee, arrive; he had taken thirty-five days to travel from Baltimore to New York. The Senate now began its official business, the first item on the agenda being the counting of the votes cast by the presidential electors. To no one's surprise, the total stood at sixty-nine electoral votes for George Washington, who therefore became the first President of the United States; John Adams, with the next highest number of votes, thirty-four, was declared Vice-president.

On April 16, Washington departed from Mount Vernon on the journey to New York City, and a few days later Senator

Morris set out for home in order to welcome the new President to Pennsylvania soil. Washington's progress was that of a hero. In Philadelphia evergreen arches were erected to shade his carriage from the sun. The most beautiful young ladies in Trenton sang songs as he passed. At Elizabethtown Point on April 23 a splendid barge, manned by thirteen men dressed as Venetian gondoliers, waited to convey the President and his entourage through a harbor crowded with colorfully decorated boats to the landing stage at New York. A jubilant crowd cheered him on the way to his quarters in Cherry Street. His journey from Virginia took only seven nights. A week later, on the balcony of Federal Hall at the corner of Wall and Broad streets, he was inaugurated.

Less than three weeks later Martha Washington, accompanied by her grandchildren, Eleanor Custis and George Washington Parke Custis, set out from Mount Vernon to join her husband. On May 23 she reached Gray's Ferry, just outside Philadelphia, where she was met by Molly Morris, other leading citizens, and a troop of soldiers, to be escorted to the Morris home on Market Street, where she rested—in between entertainments—for the weekend. The following Monday the trip was resumed, with Mrs. Morris and Maria as guests in her carriage. On Wednesday, the two husbands, one a president and the other a senator, met their wives at Elizabethtown, where they all boarded the President's barge for the trip to Manhattan.

Toward the end of May, Martha Washington gave her first reception. Here Molly Morris occupied the place of honor on her right, as she would continue to do at future receptions held by the President's wife. Robert was accorded the same honor by Washington at public and private dinners, preferential treatment that increased the enmity of his opponents.

Meanwhile, an impost bill, proposing a tax on imports, was being debated in the Senate. One Sunday Morris and Maclay had a private debate on the subject, which Morris ended by jumping up and declaring, "I want to go and take a stroll somewhere." Maclay took this impatience to indicate that his colleague "did not like close thinking," but he believed that Morris had "a strong and vigorous mind when it does act." The two men set out for a jaunt to the Narrows, but no boat could be found, so they contented themselves with walking up the bank of the North River to an acquaintance's home, where, after wandering delightedly through the greenhouse and gardens, they dined. When the impost bill was debated on the floor of the Senate and a senator from New England attacked the position of the two Pennsylvanians, Maclay reported that he could see Morris's "nostrils widen, and his nose flatten like the head of a viper."

In Paris, Gouverneur Morris was beginning to receive disturbing reports. Robert's private accounts in Europe were more snarled than the younger man had realized, and he was repeatedly reminded that his friend, in an attempt to build a financial empire, was spreading his assets thin. One of his London colleagues already was in Fleet Street prison for debt. And then came word that Dutch bankers had refused a loan on the Morris land at the Falls of Trenton, where Robert cherished the hope that the national capital would be built.

August brought Senator Morris into conflict with President Washington. On the twenty-second, Washington, accompanied by Secretary of War Henry Knox, appeared in the Senate to tell its members that he wished their advice and consent on matters pertaining to a treaty being negotiated with Indians in the South. Vice-president Adams then quickly read seven questions and after each one asked, "Do you advise and consent?" The senators remained uncomfortably silent. At last Morris rose to his feet to declare that the questions required careful study and thought; he moved that they be referred to a committee. The motion was seconded; then Maclay spoke at length. According to Maclay, Washington's impatience became increasingly evident. Finally, "in a violent fret," Washington started up and exclaimed angrily, "This defeats every purpose of my coming here." To calm his wrath, the Senate agreed to give its answers within three days.

Morris occasionally found himself also in conflict with Maclay over the rights of the states; at times Maclay feared that Morris would prefer to see a totally dominant federal government. But relations between the two were not strained to the breaking point, and Maclay often dined at the Morris residence. He thought Molly Morris to be "at least the second female character at court" and certainly "the first in taste and etiquette." Maclay, like many others, suspected Washington of aristocratic pretensions and satirically spoke of "The Republican Court."

One night, while dining at the Morrises', Maclay noted the scarcity of cream. Molly told him that her servants had searched the countryside, but no cream was to be found. Two nights before, she told Maclay, she had dined at the Washingtons', where a splendid-looking custard was served for dessert. President Washington served her a large helping, but with the first bite she raised her handkerchief to her mouth, spat the custard into it, and whispered to Washington that the custard must have been made with stale, rancid cream. Then, according to Maclay, Molly added with a titter, "Mrs. Washington ate a whole heap of it."

By now Congress had submitted the Bill of Rights to the states for ratification; not only had Henry Knox been named Secretary of War, but Thomas Jefferson had been named Secretary of State. Washington is said to have approached Morris about another important post; he reportedly remarked to his old friend, "After your invaluable services as Financier of the Revolution, no one can pretend to contest the office of the Secretary of the Treasury with you." Whether or not the post actually was offered, Morris did not want it. The time of crisis and of selfless service was past. At fifty-five, he knew that his energy was not what it had been, especially the energy needed to push controversial programs through the obstructions raised by his enemies. Even now, his business speculations needed more attention than he could give them. But, most important, Morris knew that Congress would prohibit his continuing his private business and land speculation while serving as Secretary of the Treasury; attitudes about the conflict of public and private interest had changed since the days of the American Revolution.

Although Morris did not wish to be Secretary of the Treasury, he had strong opinions about which man should hold the job that seemed second in importance only to that of the President. According to Maclay, Morris thought that Alexander Hamilton was "damned sharp"; James Madison agreed; and together they urged Hamilton's appointment. When Washington nominated Hamilton, the Senate quickly confirmed the appointment. Once Hamilton was in office, Morris supported him in every way he could, especially in proposals for a tariff and for funding national and state debts.

The question of whether or not the national government would assume the state debts became entangled with the question of where the new national capital was to be located. In late September, 1789, the House, having considered a spot on the Potomac River, sent the Senate a bill proposing a site on the banks of the Susquehanna River. Robert Morris maneuvered skillfully in the Senate. Although he had hoped to see the permanent residence of the government located on his tract of land near the Falls of Trenton, he eventually was largely responsible for the Senate's proposing a location in Germantown. As he wrote to Gouverneur:

> I have been exceedingly plagued with the question of "Permanent Residence." . . . We have been playing hide and seek on the banks of the Potomac, Susquehannah, Conegochegue, &c, &c. It has constantly been my view to bring the ramblers back to the banks of the Delaware, but the obstinacy of one or two, and the schemes of some others, prevented my getting them so high up as the Falls.

One device Morris used was to offer $100,000 on behalf of Pennsylvania to defray building expenses if the site selected was at Germantown. When Maclay challenged his authority to pledge state funds, Morris asserted that if the state did not wish to contribute he would raise the money himself.

Eventually Hamilton joined in the game. He let it be known that if Maryland would support his program for the assumption of state debts, he would exert his influence in favor of Baltimore; if Pennsylvania would support him, he would favor Germantown or the Falls. But the Pennsylvania representatives, despite Morris, insisted that Philadelphia must be the site. At last Thomas Jefferson made clear that he would back a compromise, and his compromise was the basis of the Residence Act which Congress finally passed in July, 1790: the captial was placed at Philadelphia for ten years and then permanently on the Potomac River.

The friendship between Morris and Washington had by now provoked enmities that Robert feared might injure the President. He confided to Gouverneur, ". . . observing that jealousies were beginning to take root, I have absented myself very much from his house, taking care to let him know the cause." Then Robert added, "God knows he cannot render me any service; I want nothing of him, either for myself or any of my connexions."

One reason for Morris's apparent severing of ties with Washington soon was evident. On February 8, 1790, he requested the Senate to appoint a committee to examine his conduct as financier. This action puzzled Maclay, who believed that Morris was under suspicion not for his conduct as Superintendent of Finance, but as a member of the Secret Committee; Maclay suspected that Morris's design was "to cloak his faults in the secret committee with his meritorious conduct as financier." Morris had already informed his colleague that his attendance in the Senate would be somewhat irregular because he urgently needed time to settle his accounts; Maclay agreed about the urgency "if he regards his reputation; and, in my opinion, he has left it too long at stake already."

Morris's behavior in other ways perplexed Maclay. Robert had proposed that the two speculate in lands which "he thought that he, from his connections in Europe, could sell at a dollar an acre"; according to Maclay, Morris favored "what the speculators call *dodging*: selling the land in Europe before he buys it here." The enterprise, Maclay thought, would place both men in jeopardy.

In December, 1790, Congress began its sessions once again in

Philadelphia, where Washington took up his residence in the Morris home at 190 Market Street. The Morrises moved next door to the house once owned by the Loyalist, Joseph Galloway, a house from which the radical Charles Willson Peale had dragged the protesting Mrs. Galloway when the property—along with the property of other Loyalists—was confiscated by Pennsylvania.

By now Maclay was not the only one aghast at Morris's speculations in land. Goueverneur, still in France, wrote that he was "sick at heart" with apprehension that Robert should "fall during my absence"; he urged his friend "to wind up some concerns *even with a loss....*"

But Robert Morris would heed no advice urging caution. All his life he had maneuvered daringly, even recklessly; he was not inclined to change his methods. Already he was wealthy, but his ambition was to become the wealthiest man in America. To obtain working capital, he divested himself of many of his mercantile interests; he also refused re-election to the Senate.

His manipulations were dazzling—for a while. In 1790 he bought a million acres in western New York; by the following year he had sold most of this tract at a profit of nearly $60,000 through his agent in London. In 1791 he bought an additional four million acres and then sold all but a half million to the Holland Company, a firm of Dutch capitalists. In 1794, with John Nicholson of Philadelphia, once the Comptroller-General of Pennsylvania, he purchased a million acres along the Susquehanna River, where he built the town of Asylum; in 1795 he sold his share to Nicholson. In 1795, with Nicholson and the rascally James Greenleaf of New York, once the American consul at Amsterdam, he formed the North American Land Company, which soon owned more than six million acres in Pennsylvania, Virginia, the Carolinas, Kentucky, and Georgia.

The Federal City on the Potomac River had been laid out in 1792; in 1793 and 1794 Morris, Nicholson, and Greenleaf bought more than seven thousand building lots there, on which they agreed to erect annually twenty brick houses, two stories high and each covering twelve hundred square feet.

Frenetically Morris tried to promote schemes to develop the wild lands he had purchased; he used all his considerable skill to persuade settlers to emigrate to his wilderness. But the prospective settlers were reluctant, surveys were expensive, and negotiations with the Indians over disputed claims did not progress as smoothly as he had anticipated.

In addition to the heavy burdens he had incurred by overextending his resources through purchases of land, Morris was dealt a severe blow by the failure of his London bank in 1793. He lost £124,000. Increasingly creditors in Europe and America clamored for payment.

His family was proving a source of both joy and sorrow. In 1795 twenty-five-year-old Robert, Jr., still in charge of his father's concerns at Morrisville, married "a charming and amiable young woman. . . ." Hetty, now twenty, married James Marshall, a Virginia lawyer, whose elder brother John would be Secretary of State and Chief Justice of the Supreme Court. James, appointed secretary of the North American Land Company, was immediately sent abroad to do what he could to sell some of Morris's vast land holdings. Thomas, in New York, was busily negotiating a treaty with the Indians. Both Robert, Jr., and Thomas seemed to be living up to the promise of their European education.

But William and Charles, both educated at the University of Pennsylvania, did not fare so admirably. William, sent to France in 1794 at twenty-one to assist Gouverneur Morris, let his family know where he was and what he was doing only through his drafts for money; although Morris called him home to supervise the holdings in the Federal City, William refused to leave Europe. Early in 1796 the distraught father wrote, "I will do anything for him except furnish him money, and will do that if I must." Soon Morris told Marshall not to lend William any money "unless it be to send him home."

In 1795, Charles, now eighteen, was apprenticed to a Philadelphia merchant; he proved such an unsatisfactory apprentice that Morris was obliged to take him into his own countinghouse, where the father hoped to train him to be "a useful and respectable member of society." But Charles, "running riot again," left home for New York. Morris, asking Thomas not to aid him, said, "I will not pay his debts nor do anything for him until he makes submission and amendment."

Meanwhile, speculation followed upon speculation. Taxes were due; mortgages were due. On paper, Morris still had a huge fortune, but almost no land could be sold or investors obtained to provide ready money.

Morris's affairs had reached such a state that President Washington was forced to rebuke him. In July, 1795, he wrote to Secretary of State Edmund Randolph that he should tell Morris and Nicholson "in earnest and strong terms" that serious consequences would result to the public buildings in the Federal City "if the deficiency, or part thereof, due on their contract, is not paid." And in September, Washington wrote directly to Morris; his motives, he said, sprang "as much from private friendship, as they do from a sense of public duty." Urging Morris to pay what was due on his contracts, Washington pointed out that many valuable men would be thrown out of work if Morris failed to meet his obligations. And with concern the President reported that rumors were circulating that Morris had taken the lots purely for speculation.

Ten days before Christmas Morris confessed to Hamilton: "I want ready money sadly but it is not want of property." Yet property could be sold only at a great sacrifice. "I do not like to sacrifice if I can help it, because I have worked hard to get what I have, and will fight a good battle to keep it." And early in 1796 the speculator informed Benjamin Harrison, "I am, as you say, beating hard up against wind and tide, and I fear I shall be obliged to have recourse to steam to get along (for I am building a steam engine at Morrisville.)"

In September, 1796, Morris spent ten weeks in the Federal City in an attempt to bring order to his chaotic affairs there. On his return journey he was thrown from his horse, an omen of a greater fall that he was soon to take.

X

From "Castle Defiance" to the Prune Street Jail

Even Morris's friends had begun to think he had gone mad. As treasurer for a bankrupt nation he had audaciously resorted to devices which kept the money machine going; when hard money was lacking, he staved off national disaster by pledging his personal credit, by using his personal notes as currency, by snaring loans when no more loans seemed possible. He grew proud; infatuated with his success, he began to see himself capable of anything, so powerful that he was indestructible. Now, as a private citizen, he had resorted to similar free-wheeling maneuvers. But he was beginning to discover that fighting to save a private empire was different from fighting to save a new nation. The power, the indestructibility, had belonged to the nation he represented, not to the individual he was.

He was constructing a monument to his magnificence on the block in Philadelphia bounded by Seventh, Chestnut, Eighth, and Walnut streets, a mansion designed by Pierre L'Enfant, who had laid out the plans for the Federal City. L'Enfant made the house more splendid than even Morris had anticipated—and more expensive. L'Enfant estimated the cost at a mere $60,000; when work was halted in 1791, with the building still unfinished, Morris was reported to have spent nearly $1,000,000. The two-story brick house was to cover almost the entire front of the square; imported marble was to decorate the porticos, doorways, and window frames.

Morris desperately tried to satisfy his creditors, "hungry as the devil." Every day, he said, he tumbled "hogsheads of sugar, bills of exchange, and paper money down their throats. . . . But all won't do unless a fresh supply comes soon." Philadelphia was experiencing a financial panic; 150 businesses failed, and more than sixty merchants were jailed for debt. By April, 1797, Gouverneur, still in France, had heard that his friend was ruined: "A heavy stroke upon my bosom, and I fear the account is but too true."

Affairs had grown so bad that by the summer of 1797, Morris and Nicholson, taking refuge at "The Hills," turned it into a fortress, which Robert nicknamed "Castle Defiance." There, Morris said, the two men did "penance for our sins." Creditors, lawyers, constables, bailiffs besieged the estate; when cold weather came, they built bonfires on the lawn. James, the gardener, did his best to protect his employer by warning him of traps that lay in wait; in November, for example, he told Robert that two creditors lurked in "Blackbeard's Hole," a quarry on the grounds. Robert swore to let no one in the house and not to go outside; "when I sniff in the open air, it is at the top. Do I write like a man in distress or one deranged? Perhaps I am both." Occasionally he would open a window to talk with a creditor, or he would look through a peephole at those hounding him: "I have been busy this morning watching the man who is watching me."

Nicholson left to return to his family; Morris's letters to him reveal the agony of the besieged man. "There is a Frenchman intends to shoot me at the window if I do not pay a note he protested on Saturday," Morris wrote. Another time he confessed, "I believe I shall go mad. Every day brings forward scenes and troubles almost unsupportable, and they seem to be accumulating so that at last they will like a torrent carry everything before them. God help us, for men will not."

A gang of six men armed with pickaxes and sledgehammers arrived to break into the fortress, but were dissuaded. Morris lamented that he was beset "with deputations, bribery, and spies, and my property selling and sacrificing everywhere, and those whose happiness I wish to promote suffering by their engagements for me." And then he added, "If ever I could have had a previous idea of such things happening to me, I would sooner have wheeled oysters all my days than incurred the risk."

Not only was his family in Philadelphia suffering, but his friends as well. Among those who lost substantial sums as a result of their involvement in Morris's ventures were Hamilton, Jay, Willing, and Bishop White, Molly's brother.

One creditor in particular, a man named Eddy, was relentless; he organized other creditors and refused to wait for payment. Some of Morris's defenders later would suggest that he might have been able to weather the crisis had not Eddy been determined to bring him down. Morris wrote his "dear Molly" that Eddy's friends were "pursuing measures to force a surrender of myself. How this may end I cannot tell, but as I am in danger, I apprise you of it, that you may be prepared to act with that fortitude which your good sense will enable you to see is proper in every event."

By February 15, Morris's fate was determined. Morris informed Nicholson, "I am here in custody of a sheriff's officer in my own house." Eddy, he stated, "was positively determined to carry me to Pruën street last night, but the sheriff humanely relieved me from his rascally clutches." On the following day the once great merchant and financier was conveyed to the Prune Street jail, where debtors were incarcerated. At first Morris had to share quarters with other prisoners; "I feel like an intruder everywhere; sleeping in other people's beds and sitting in other people's rooms, I am writing on other people's paper, with other people's ink. . . ." He remarked bitterly, as other debtors had remarked, "If my creditors were wise for their own sakes, they would not keep me idle here, when, if I had my liberty, I might work efficiently for their benefit."

Eventually he secured a room for himself, even though the rates were high and he had to borrow even "market money" to provide for his family. He revealed to friends that he was "suffering not only the extremity of the law, but the torments of insulted sensibility." To Nicholson he wrote, "This place ought to be avoided by all that can possibly keep out of it, and I hope to God you may succeed, but I doubt it." His doubts proved correct; Nicholson was thrown into prison, where he died in December, 1880.

Morris tried to be cheerful when writing to his family. To Tom he said, "My health is good, my spirits not broke, my mind sound and vigorous, and therefore I will do all I can consistently with principles of integrity to make the best of my affairs and extricate myself as well as I can."

His son, William, who had returned from Europe to attempt to help with his father's affairs, was stricken with fever and died on October 10. Morris grieved; "his value to his family I never counted until he was lost, and now I see its magnitude, and that is irreparable." In December Morris's friend, the brilliant James Wilson, died soon after having been released from jail, where he had been dragged for drunkenness and debt.

Morris's friends did what they could. George Washington dined with him in the dingy room, cluttered with borrowed furniture; the Washingtons insisted that Molly and Maria visit with them at Mount Vernon. Mrs. John Adams went to visit Molly in 1798 and reported that she "met her without knowing her, so altered that I was shocked. Maria pale, wan, dejected & spiritless." Again in 1799, Abigail Adams visited her distressed friend; she found her in "a small neat room" at dinner with Maria and Charles; Molly tried to smile away her very evident melancholy. Gouverneur Morris, once he returned to America, frequently visited "my poor friend Robert Morris." Gouverneur tried to keep Robert and Molly "in high spirits" with "a very lively strain of conversation," but he noted that Molly "puts on an air of firmness which she cannot support."

When an epidemic of yellow fever broke out, Robert tried to

persuade Molly to move from her rented quarters, but she refused because she insisted on being near her husband in his "ugly whitewashed vault."

The unfinished mansion, dubbed "Morris's Folly," fell into decay and eventually was demolished. "The Hills" was sold at auction in 1799; bought by Henry Pratt, the house may, in a remodeled form, have survived as the handsome "Lemon Hill," which still stands in what is now Fairmount Park.

One man who saw Robert Morris in prison later recalled the impression:

> . . . he was of nearly six feet in stature; of large, full, well-formed, vigorous frame; with clear, smooth, florid complexion. His loose, gray hair was unpowdered. . . . He wore, as was common at that day, a full suit of broadcloth. . . . His manners were gracious and simple, and free from the formality which generally prevails. He was very affable, and mingled in common conversation, even with the young.

Even while Morris lay in prison, his talents were not forgotten. President Thomas Jefferson, when forming his cabinet in March, 1801, wrote to his Secretary of State, James Madison, that if Morris "could get from confinement, and the public give him confidence, he would be a most valuable officer in that station [Secretary of the Navy] and in our council."

Within six months Morris did "get from confinement." In 1800, Congress had passed an act which stated that, "on the petition of his creditors," a man could be adjudged a bankrupt and thus released from prison. After three years, six months, and ten days in the Prune Street jail, the man who had almost become the wealthiest man in America was released on August 26, 1801. "I now find myself a free citizen of the United States," he said, "without one cent that I can call my own." But, as he wrote to Tom the next day, "I had the inexpressible satisfaction to find myself again restored to my home and family."

"Home" was a modest residence on Twelfth Street, between Market and Chestnut, where Molly had taken quarters on an annuity of $1,500 that Gouverneur had managed to salvage for her. Gouverneur persuaded Robert to visit him at Morrisania during the summer of 1802; Robert arrived, "lean, low-spirited, and as poor as a commission of bankruptcy can make a man whose effects will, it is said, not pay a shilling in the pound." When Robert left, Gouverneur reported, he was "fat, sleek, in good spirits and possessed of the means for living comfortably the rest of his days." The generous Gouverneur, of course, had provided the "means."

The rest of Robert Morris's days were to be few; he died on May 8, 1806, and was buried in Christ Churchyard in Philadelphia. Molly lingered on in relative obscurity until January 16, 1827.

When Robert Morris died, his reputation had been corroded by his spectacular bankruptcy and his years in debtors' prison; fame looks acidly on a financial failure. As the decades have passed, however, the magnitude of his achievement increasingly has emerged from beneath the blotched surface of his dismal last years.

Although Morris's progress was scarcely one from rags to riches, his beginnings were modest and his schooling was haphazard. Through ceaseless hard work, intelligence, shrewdness, and ingenuity, he rose to be Prince of Merchants, a pioneer in the trade with China, and eventually—although briefly—to be one of the wealthiest men in America. He was, in fact, one of the first of an American type: the modern businessman.

But his exploits as businessman are secondary to his accomplishments as statesman and patriot. He signed and then vigorously supported the three most important documents of the nation's early years—the Declaration of Independence, the Articles of Confederation, and the Constitution (Roger Sherman was the only other man to sign all three); and Morris served in the first United States Senate.

As Superintendent of Finance, Morris contributed significantly to the victory of the troops under Washington. His influence during the final years of the Revolution was, as historian E. James Ferguson has said, "probably greater than that of any other man except Washington.... During his administration he managed to commit the United States to a course of action that sustained national unity in the postwar years and led, eventually, to the movement for the Constitution and the enactment of the Hamiltonian funding program."

Morris, during his career, provoked the virulence of such men as Tom Paine, Arthur Lee, Joseph Reed, and others; but he also inspired respect, admiration, and friendship in others—Gouverneur Morris, John Jay, Alexander Hamilton, and George Washington among them.

In the last decade of his life Morris overreached himself, and the debacle was complete. But that very quality of reckless daring contributed significantly to his success in aiding the struggle to win—and maintain—independence.

Bibliography

I. PRIMARY MATERIAL ON ROBERT MORRIS

Adams, Abigail. *New Letters of Abigail Adams: 1788–1801.* Edited by Stewart Mitchell. Boston: Houghton Mifflin Company, 1947.

Adams, John. *Diary and Autobiography of John Adams.* (Vols. 1–4 in Series I of The Adams Papers, L. H. Butterfield, Editor-in-Chief.) Cambridge, Mass: Harvard University Press, 1961.

———. *The Works of John Adams, Second President of the United States.* Edited by Charles Francis Adams. 10 vols. Boston: Little, Brown and Company, 1856.

Adams, John and Abigail. *Familiar Letters of John Adams and His Wife Abigail Adams During the Revolution.* Edited by Charles Francis Adams. New York: Hurd and Houghton, 1876.

Adams, John and Abigail et al. *Adams Family Correspondence.* (Vols. 1–2 in Series II of The Adams Papers, L. H. Butterfield, Editor-in-Chief.) Cambridge, Mass.: Harvard University Press, 1963.

Adams, John and Abigail, and Jefferson, Thomas. *The Adams-Jefferson Letters: The Complete Correspondence Between Thomas Jefferson and Abigail and John Adams.* Edited by Lester J. Capon. 2 vols. Chapel Hill: The University of North Carolina Press, 1959.

Banning, Jeremiah. "Narrative of the Principal Incident in the Life of Jeremiah Banning. Written by Himself in 1793." *Boogher's Repository*, Vol. I (1883).

Breck, Samuel. *Recollections of Samuel Breck.* Edited by H. E. Scudder. Philadelphia: Porter and Coates, 1877.

Burnett, Edmund C., Editor. *Letters of Members of the Continental Congress.* 8 vols. Washington, D. C.: Carnegie Institution of Washington, 1921–1936.

Champion, Richard. *The American Correspondence of a Bristol Merchant: Letters of Richard Champion.* Edited by G. H. Guttridge. California University Publications in History, Vol. XXII, No. 1. Berkeley, Calif.: University of California Press, 1934.

Clark, William Bell, Editor. *Naval Documents of the American Revolution.* Vol. I. Washington, D. C.: U. S. Government Printing Office, 1964.

Hamilton, Alexander. *The Papers of Alexander Hamilton.* Edited by Harold C. Syrett et al. Vols. I- . New York: Columbia University Press, 1961- .

Hart, Charles Henry, Editor. "Mrs. John Jay to Mrs. Robert Morris." *Boogher's Repository,* Vol. I (1883).

Henkels, Stanislaus Vincent, Editor. *The Confidential Correspondence of Robert Morris.* Catalogue No. 1183. Philadelphia, 1917.

Homes, Henry A. *Description and Analysis of the Remarkable Collection of Unpublished Manuscripts of Robert Morris.* Albany: Joel Munsell, 1876.

Jay, John. *The Correspondence and Public Papers of John Jay.* Edited by Henry P. Johnston. 4 vols. New York: G. P. Putnam's Sons, 1890-1893.

Maclay, William. *The Journal of William Maclay.* Edited by Edgar Maclay. New York: Albert and Charles Boni, 1927.

———. *Sketches of Debate in the First Senate of the United States.* Harrisburg, Pa.: Printed by Lane S. Hart, 1880.

Marshall, Christopher. *Passages from the Remembrancer of Christopher Marshall.* Edited by William Duane, Jr. Philadelphia: Printed by James Crissy, 1839.

Morris, Gouverneur. *Diary and Letters of Gouverneur Morris.* Edited by Anne Cary Morris. 2 vols. London: Keegan Paul, Trench, 1889.

Morris, Robert. *Account of Robert Morris' Property.* n.d.

———. Manuscript Letters in the Cadwallader, Dreer, Etting, Franklin, Gratz, Society, and Wayne Collections of the Historical Society of Pennsylvania.

———. *The Papers of Robert Morris, 1781-1784.* Edited by E. James Ferguson et al. Vols. I- . Pittsburgh: University of Pittsburgh Press, 1973- .

New-York Historical Society. *Collections.* Publication Fund Series: Vols. XI (1879), XIX (1887), XX (1888), XXI (1889). New York: Published for the Society.

Reed, William B. *Life and Correspondence of Joseph Reed.* 2 vols. Philadelphia: Lindsay and Blakiston, 1847.

Sparks, Jared, Editor. *Correspondence of the American Revolution.* 4 vols. Boston: Little, Brown and Company, 1853.

———. *The Diplomatic Correspondence of the American Revolution.* 12 vols. Boston: Nathan Hale and Gray and Bowen, 1830.

Thacher, James. *A Military Journal During the American Revolutionary War.* Boston: Richardson and Lord, 1823.
Washington, George. *The Writings of George Washington.* Edited by John C. Fitzpatrick. 39 vols. Washington, D. C.: U. S. Government Printing Office, 1931-1944.
Wharton, Francis, Editor. *The Revolutionary Diplomatic Correspondence of the United States.* 6 vols. Washington, D. C.: U. S. Government Printing Office, 1889.

II. SECONDARY MATERIAL ON ROBERT MORRIS

Alberts, Robert C. *The Golden Voyage: The Life and Times of William Bingham.* Boston: Houghton Mifflin Company, 1969.
Augur, Helen. *The Secret War of Independence.* New York and Boston: Little, Brown and Company, 1955.
Burnett, Edmund Cody. *The Continental Congress.* New York: The Macmillan Company, 1942.
Clark, William Bell. "The John Ashmead Story." *The Pennsylvania Magazine of History and Biography.* LXXXII (1958), 3-54.
Dangerfield, George. *Chancellor Robert R. Livingston of New York.* New York: Harcourt, Brace and Company, 1960.
Eberlein, Harold D., and Hubbard, C. V. D. *Diary of Independence Hall.* Philadelphia: Lippincott, 1948.
Ferguson, E. James. *The Power of the Purse: A History of American Public Finance, 1776-1790.* Chapel Hill, N. C.: The University of North Carolina Press, 1961.
Griswold, Rufus Wilmot. *The Republican Court, or American Society in the Days of Washington.* New York: Appleton, 1856.
Hart, Charles Henry. *Mary White—Mrs. Robert Morris—An Address.* Philadelphia: 1878.
———. *Robert Morris, the Financier of the American Revolution—A Sketch.* Philadelphia: Collins, Printer, 1878.
Hastings. George Everett. *The Life and Works of Francis Hopkinson.* Chicago: The University of Chicago Press, 1926.
Hatch, Louis C. *The Administration of the American Revolutionary Army.* New York: Longmans, Green, and Company, 1904.
Hawke, David Freeman. *Paine.* New York: Harper and Row, Publishers, 1974.
Herring, James, and Longacre, James B. *The National Portrait Gallery of Distinguished Americans.* 5 vols. Philadelphia: Robert E. Peterson and Company, 1852-1867.
Hunt, Freeman. *Lives of American Merchants.* 2 vols. New York: Derby and Jackson, 1858.
Johnson, Victor L. "Robert Morris and the Provisioning of the American Army During the Campaign of 1781." *Pennsylvania History,* V (January, 1938), 7-20.

Kennedy, John. *The Genessee Country.* Batavia, N. Y.: Calkins and Lent, 1895.
———. *Robert Morris and the Holland Purchase.* Batavia, N. Y.: J. F. Hall, 1894.
Konkle, Burton Alva. *Thomas Willing and the First American Financial System.* Philadelphia: University of Pennsylvania Press, 1937.
Lewis, Lawrence, Jr. *A History of the Bank of North America.* Philadelphia: Lippincott, 1882.
Main, Jackson Turner. *The Antifederalists: Critics of the Constitution, 1781–1788.* Chapel Hill, N. C.: The University of North Carolina Press, 1961.
Morris, Richard B. *Seven Who Shaped Our Destiny.* New York: Harper and Row, Publishers, 1973.
Oberholtzer, Ellis Paxson. *Philadelphia: A History of the City and Its People.* Philadelphia: The S. J. Clarke Publishing Company, 1912.
———. *Robert Morris: Patriot and Financier.* New York: The Macmillan Company, 1903.
Rossiter, Clinton. *1787: The Grand Convention.* New York: The Macmillan Company, 1966.
Sanderson, John. *Sanderson's Biography of the Signers of the Declaration of Independence.* Revised and edited by Robert J. Conrad. Philadelphia: Thomas, Cowperthwaite and Company, 1847.
Scharf, J. Thomas, and Westcott, Thompson. *History of Philadelphia.* 3 vols. Philadelphia: L. H. Everts and Company, 1884.
Simpson, Henry. *The Lives of Eminent Philadelphians.* Philadelphia: William Brotherhead, 1859.
Smith, C. Page. "The Attack on Fort Wilson." *The Pennsylvania Magazine of History and Biography,* LXXVIII (April, 1954), 177–188.
———. *James Wilson, Founding Father.* Chapel Hill, N. C.: The University of North Carolina Press, 1956.
Sparks, Jared. *The Life of Gouverneur Morris.* 3 vols. Boston: Gray and Bowen, 1832.
Sumner, William Graham. *The Financier and the Finances of the American Revolution.* 2 vols. New York: Dodd, Mead, and Company, 1891.
———. *Robert Morris.* New York: Dodd, Mead, and Company, 1892.
Swiggett, Howard. *The Extraordinary Mr. Morris.* Garden City, N. Y.: Doubleday and Company, Inc., 1952.
Thayer, Theodore. *Nathanael Greene.* New York: Twayne Publishers, 1960.
Ver Steeg, Clarence L. *Robert Morris, Revolutionary Financier.* Philadelphia: University of Pennsylvania Press, 1954.
Wharton, Anne Hollingsworth. *Salons, Colonial and Republican.* Philadelphia: Lippincott, 1900.
———. *Through Colonial Doorways.* Philadelphia: Lippincott, 1893.

Young, Eleanor. *Forgotten Patriot: Robert Morris.* New York: The Macmillan Company, 1950.

III. BACKGROUND MATERIAL ON PHILADELPHIA, THE COMING OF THE REVOLUTION, AND THE ERA OF THE REVOLUTION

Aldridge, Alfred Owen. *Benjamin Franklin, Philosopher and Man.* Philadelphia: Lippincott, 1965.

Bowen, Catherine Drinker. *Miracle at Philadelphia: The Story of the Constitutional Convention, May to September 1787.* Boston: Little, Brown and Company, 1966.

Burnaby, Andrew. *Travels Through the Middle Settlements in North-America.* Ithaca, N. Y.: Cornell University Press, 1960.

Bridenbaugh, Carl. *Cities in Revolt: Urban Life in America, 1743–1776.* New York: Alfred A. Knopf, 1955.

Bridenbaugh, Carl and Jessica. *Rebels and Gentlemen: Philadelphia in the Age of Franklin.* New York: Reynal and Hitchcock, 1942.

Chastellux, Marquis de. *Travels in North America in the Years 1780, 1781, and 1782.* 2 vols. Chapel Hill, N. C.: The University of North Carolina Press, 1963.

Defoe, Daniel. *A Tour Through the Whole Island of Great Britain.* 2 vols. New York: Dutton, 1962.

Dos Passos, John. *The Men Who Made the Nation.* Garden City, N. Y.: Doubleday and Company, Inc., 1957.

Eberlein, Harold D., and Hubbard, C. V. D. *Portrait of a Colonial City.* Philadelphia: Lippincott, 1939.

Faris, John T. *The Romance of Old Philadelphia.* Philadelphia: Lippincott, 1918.

Flexner, James Thomas. *George Washington and the New Nation.* Boston: Little, Brown and Company, 1970.

Forbes, Esther. *Paul Revere & the World He Lived In.* Boston: Houghton Mifflin Company, 1942.

Gipson, Lawrence Henry. *The Coming of the Revolution, 1763–1775.* New York: Harper and Brothers, 1954.

Handlin, Oscar. *The Americans: A New History of the People of the United States.* Boston: Little, Brown and Company, 1963.

Hazleton, John. *The Declaration of Independence.* New York: Dodd, Mead and Company, 1906.

Jackson, Joseph. *America's Most Historic Highway: Market Street, Philadelphia.* New Edition. Philadelphia and New York: John Wanamaker, 1926.

———. *Encyclopedia of Philadelphia.* 4 vols. Harrisburg, Pa.: The National Historical Association, 1931–1933.

Maier, Pauline. *From Resistance to Revolution: Colonial Radicals and the Development of American Opposition to Britain, 1765–1776.* New York: Alfred A. Knopf, 1972.

Main, Jackson Turner. *The Sovereign States, 1775–1783.* New York: Franklin Watts, 1973.
Miller, John C. *Alexander Hamilton: Portrait in Paradox.* New York: Harper and Brothers, Publishers, 1959.
———. *The Federalist Era, 1789–1801.* New York: Harper and Brothers, Publishers, 1960.
Morison, Samuel Eliot. *John Paul Jones.* Boston: Little, Brown and Company, 1959.
Morris, Richard B., Editor. *Encyclopedia of American History.* Revised and Enlarged Edition. New York: Harper and Brothers, Publishers, 1961.
Morris, Richard B. *The Peacemakers: The Great Powers and American Independence.* New York: Harper and Row, Publishers, 1965.
Paullin, Charles Oscar. *The Navy of the American Revolution.* Cleveland: The Burrows Brothers Company, 1906.
Russell, Charles Edward. *Haym Salomon and the Revolution.* New York: Cosmopolitan Book Corporation, 1930.
Scheer, George F., and Rankin, Hugh F. *Rebels and Redcoats.* Cleveland: The World Publishing Company, 1957.
Schlesinger, Arthur M. *Prelude to Independence: The Newspaper War on Britain, 1764–1776.* New York: Alfred A. Knopf, 1958.
Smith, Page. *John Adams.* 2 vols. Garden City, N. Y.: Doubleday and Company, Inc., 1962.
Van Doren, Carl. *Benjamin Franklin.* New York: Garden City Publishing Company, 1941.
Wallace, David Duncan. *The Life of Henry Laurens.* New York: G. P. Putnam's Sons, 1915.
Wallace, Willard M. *Traitorous Hero: The Life and Fortunes of Benedict Arnold.* New York: Harper and Brothers, Publishers, 1954.
Ward, Christopher. *The War of the Revolution.* Edited by John Richard Alden. 2 vols. New York: The Macmillan Company, 1952.
Watson, John F. *Annals of Philadelphia.* Philadelphia: E. L. Carey and A. Hart, 1830.
Wechsburg, Joseph. *The Merchant Bankers.* Boston: Little, Brown and Company, 1966.
Young, John Russell. *Memorial History of the City of Philadelphia.* 2 vols. New York: New-York History Company, 1895–1898.

Index

Acadians, 11
Adams, Abigail, 45, 131
Adams, John, 27-30, 32, 45, 54, 93, 105, 118, 120
Adams, Samuel, 25, 27-28, 32, 76
Agent of Marine. *See* Morris, Robert
Allen, Ethan, 27
Alliance, 108
America (*Le Franklin*), 85
Andrew Doria, 36
Annapolis Convention. *See* Convention, Annapolis
Army, British, 26, 33, 37-38, 43, 45-47, 49, 52-53, 57, 79, 81-82
Army, Continental, 33-34, 36, 38-39, 41-42, 45-47, 52, 57, 75-76, 78-81, 93-94, 97, 100-104, 133
Army, French, 8-13, 80-81
Arnold, Benedict, 27, 52, 58, 88, 108
Arnold, Margaret Shippen, 58
Articles of Confederation, 44, 47-48, 92, 109-110, 112, 133
Assembly, Pennsylvania, 10, 19, 24, 27, 42, 53, 56, 58, 107-108, 118
Asylum, Pennsylvania, 124
Ayres, Captain, 23-24

Baltimore, Maryland, 33-34, 38-39, 41, 43, 80, 84, 118, 123
Bank of North America, 78, 88-89, 102-103, 107-108
Bank of Pennsylvania, 57, 78
Banning, Jeremiah, 4

Barbé-Marbois, François, 109
Barry, John, 108
Battle of the Wilderness, 10
Bell, Thomas, 53
Bill of Rights, 121
Bingham, Anne Willing, 41
Bingham, William, 40-41, 52, 57, 88
Boston, Massachusetts, 11, 18, 20, 22-25, 48, 85
Boston Port Bill, 24-25
Boston Tea Party, 23-24
Boudinot, Elias, 103-104
Braddock, Edward, 10
Brandywine Creek, 46
Broglie, Charles François, Comte de, 95
Brown, John, 49
Burgoyne, John, 47
Burke, Thomas, 46
Burnaby, Andrew, 14

Cadwallader, John, 55
Camden, South Carolina, 57
Campbell, Robert, 56
Canada, 9, 13
Canton, China, 105, 108
Carleton, Sir Guy, 93
"Castle, The," 47
"Castle Defiance," 129-130
"Centinel," 115-116
Charleston, South Carolina, 22, 57, 82
Chastellux, François Jean, Marquis de, 80

141

Index

Chesapeake Bay, 3, 45, 79
Chester, Delaware, 23
Christ Church, 17, 133
City Tavern, 26, 80, 88, 111-112, 114
Clark, Abraham, 32
Clinton, Sir Henry, 52, 57-58, 79, 88, 93
Clymer, George, 34
College Hall, 52, 111
College of Philadelphia. *See* University of Pennsylvania
Committee of Safety, Pennsylvania, 27
Committee of Secret Correspondence, 27-28, 40
Common Sense, 29
Concord, Massachusetts, 26
Congress, First Continental, 25,
Congress, Second Continental, 27-35, 37-38, 40-44, 46-50, 52-55, 75-79, 82, 84, 89-92, 96-99, 101-106, 109, 111, 114, 117
Congress, United States, 118, 121, 132. *See also* House of Representatives; Senate, United States
Connecticut Compromise (The Great Compromise), 113
Constable, William, 118
Constitution, United States, 113-118, 133-134
Convention, Annapolis, 109-110
Convention, Constitutional, 110-114
Cornwallis, Charles, 2d Earl and 1st Marquis Cornwallis, 38, 79, 81
Council of Safety, Pennsylvania, 49
Cuba, 12
Currency, Continental, 35, 75, 90. *See also* "Morris Notes"
Custis, Eleanor, 119
Custis, George Washington Parke, 119

Deane, Silas, 28, 33-35, 39-40, 44-45, 49-50, 54, 87-88
Declaration of Independence, 29-32, 49, 56, 133
Defoe, Daniel, 1-2
Delaware River, 5, 8, 16-17, 19, 21, 23, 27, 33, 36, 52, 81
Dickinson, John, 24, 30, 47, 103
Dieskau, Ludwig August, Baron von, 10
Dobbs Ferry, New York, 80
Dock Creek Harbor, 5

East India Company, 22-24
Eddy, George, 130

Elizabethtown Point, New Jersey, 119
Empress of China, 105
England, 1, 6, 8, 13-15, 19, 22, 25-26, 28-29, 35, 52, 88, 100. *See also* London, England

Falls of Trenton, 117, 120, 122-123
Farmers-General, 108, 117
Federal City (Washington, District of Columbia), 124-128
Federal Hall, 119
Federalists, 115-116
Ferguson, E. James, 134
Financier's Report on Public Credit, 92
Fort Cumberland, 10
Fort Duquesne, 10
Fort Necessity, 9
Fort Ticonderoga, 27
"Fort Wilson," 56
Foster Cunliffe and Sons, 1-3, 6
France, 28, 33, 39, 49-52, 75, 77, 79, 84-85, 88, 92-93, 101, 108, 117, 124, 125, 129. *See also* French and Indian War; Paris, France
Francis, Tench, Jr., 57
Franklin, Benjamin, 27-30, 33-35, 39, 45, 50, 56, 77-79, 8⁄ 88, 93, 102, 105, 110, 112
French and Indian Wars, 9-13

Galloway, Joseph, 48, 124
Gates, Horatio, 47
Geneva, Switzerland, 84
George II, 8, 15
George III, 15, 17, 20, 25-26, 31
Germantown, Pennsylvania, 15, 122-123
Grasse, François Joseph Paul, Comte de, 79, 81, 83-84
Great Britain. *See* England
Greene, Nathanael, 78, 91, 94, 98-99
Greenleaf, James, 124
Greenway, Robert, 4-6

Hall, Jemmy, 44
Hall, Sophia, 34
Hamilton, Alexander, 14-15, 57-58, 78, 86, 91, 96, 99, 101-102, 104, 113, 122, 126, 130, 134
Hamilton's Wharf, 5
Hancock, John, 31, 34, 41-43, 48
Harrison, Benjamin, 27-28, 30, 39, 126
Head of Elk (Elkton), Maryland, 81
Henry, Patrick, 27, 116

Index 143

Hessians, 36, 47
"Hills, The," 21, 25, 47, 53, 56, 75, 80, 110, 112, 129-130, 132
Holker, John, 55, 108
Holland, 93, 96, 105, 120
Holland Company, 124
House, Mary, 110
House of Representatives, 113, 118, 122
Howe, Richard, 4th Viscount and 1st Earl Howe, 33-34
Howe, Sir William, 5th Viscount Howe, 33-34, 43, 45-49, 52, 108
Hughes, John, 18
Humphreys, Charles, 30
Huntington, Samuel, 76

Import duties, 92, 102, 119-120
Indian Queen Tavern, 112
Indians, treaties with, 120, 125

Jamaica, 11-12, 42
Jay, John, 28, 54, 75, 79, 84, 93, 103, 105, 130, 134
Jay, Sarah, 56-57, 75, 84
Jefferson, Thomas, 28, 30-31, 94, 121, 123, 132
Johnson, Sir William, 10
Jones, John Paul, 42, 51, 53, 85

Kingston, Jamaica, 12
Knox, Henry, 120-121

Lafayette, Marie Joseph Paul, Marquis de, 79, 88
Lake George, 10
Lancaster, Pennsylvania, 36, 46-47, 103-104
Laurens, Henry, 50, 54
Lee, Arthur, 28, 33-35, 39, 45, 92, 115, 134
Lee, Richard Henry, 27-29, 118
Lee, William, 105
"Lemon Hill." *See* "Hills, The"
L'Enfant, Pierre, 128
Lexington, Massachusetts, 26
Liverpool, England, 1-2
Livingston, Robert, 29
London, England, 120, 124-125
London Coffee House, 13, 19, 26, 82
Louis XVI, 109
Loyalists, 37, 46, 48, 124
"Lucius," 99-100
Luzerne, Chevalier Anne César de la, 75, 93, 95-96, 102

McDougall, Alexander, 97
Maclay, William, 118-124
Maclayville (Harrisburg), Pennsylvania, 118
Madison, James, 94-95, 98-99, 101, 110, 112, 116, 122, 132
Manheim, Pennsylvania, 47-49, 53
Marbois. *See* Barbé-Marbois, François
Marie Antoinette, 109
Marine Committee, 28, 53
Marine Office, 78, 84-85, 92
Marshall, Christopher, 24
Marshall, James, 125
Marshall, John, 125
Martinique, 40, 57
Mifflin, Thomas, 54-56
Minerva, 19
Mint, United States, 90
Mississippi River, 42
Monmouth, New Jersey, 52
Moore, Jane, 112
Morris, Charles, 47, 117, 125-126, 131
Morris, Gouverneur, 76, 87, 90, 93, 97, 99, 104, 108, 112-114, 116-117, 120, 122-125, 129, 131, 133-134
Morris, Henry, 117
Morris, Hetty, 25, 34, 44, 47, 117, 125
Morris, Maria, 53, 58, 119, 131
Morris, Mary White, 21, 25, 34, 38, 44, 47, 53, 58, 75, 80, 83, 95, 103, 108, 110-112, 117, 119, 121, 130-133
Morris, Robert (Superintendent of Finance), birth and childhood in Liverpool, 1-2; sails to America, 1-3; lives with father in Maryland, 3-4; moves to Philadelphia, 4-5; apprenticed to Charles Willing, 5-9; death of father, 6-7; sails to Jamaica and Cuba, 11-12; partnership with Thomas Willing, 12-16, 18-19, 22-25, 28, 40-41, 47-48, 53-54; protests Stamp Act, 17-20; marries Mary White, 21; birth of children, 21, 25, 47, 53, 117; builds "The Hills," 21; protests Tea Act, 22-24; appointed to Committee of Safety, 27; elected to Pennsylvania Assembly, 27-30, 53, 74-75; member of Second Continental Congress, 27-48; member of Secret Committee and Committee of Secret Correspondence, 27-28, 33, 35, 41, 48-49, 53-54; member of Marine Committee, 28, 35, 41; opposes Declaration of Independence, 31; signs Declaration, 32; relations with

Morris, Robert (*continued*)
half brother, 32-33, 44-45, 49-51; manages Congressional affairs in Philadelphia, 34-43; moves with Congress to York, 47; signs Articles of Confederation, 48; receives leave of absence from Congress, 48; controversy with Tom Paine, 54-55; attacked by mob at "Fort Wilson," 56; helps establish Bank of Pennsylvania, 57; appointed Superintendent of Finance, 76-77; activities as Superintendent, 78-81, 86-94, 97-106; visits Washington's headquarters, 80; raises money and provisions for Yorktown, 80-81; sends elder sons to Europe, 83-84; acts as Agent of Marine, 84-85; organizes Bank of North America, 78, 88-89; issues "Morris Notes," 90; urges establishment of mint, 90; sends Financier's Report on Public Credit to Congress, 92; resigns as Superintendent, 98-99; attacked by "Lucius," 99-100; flees with Congress to Princeton, 104; sends *Empress of China* to Canton, 105; fights to save Bank of North America, 107-108; deals with Farmers-General, 108; sends *Alliance* to Canton, 108; buys home at 190 High Street, 108-109; attends Annapolis Convention, 110; member of Constitutional Convention, 110-114; attacked by "Centinel," 115-116; serves as United States Senator, 118-123; speculates in land, 123-127; starts building mansion, 128-129; besieged by creditors, 129-130; imprisoned in Prune Street jail, 130-132; visits Gouverneur Morris, 133; dies, 133; achievements, 133-134
Morris, Robert, Jr., 21, 34, 44, 83-84, 113, 117, 125
Morris, Robert, Sr., 1, 3-4, 6-7
Morris, Thomas, 21, 34, 44, 47, 83-84, 113, 117, 125, 131-132
Morris, Thomas Wise, 7, 32-33, 44-45, 49-52, 54
Morris, William, 21, 34, 44, 117, 125, 131
"Morris notes," 90, 102-103, 106
Morrisania, New York, 76, 133
"Morris's Folly," 128, 132
Morristown, New Jersey, 38, 42, 57, 75
Morrisville, Pennsylvania, 117, 125-126
Morton, John, 30

Morton, Robert, 46
Mount Vernon, 108-109, 117-119, 131

Navy, British, 33-35, 39, 42, 45, 49, 52
Navy, Continental, 34, 36, 41-42, 85
Navy, French, 52, 55, 81
New Brunswick, New Jersey, 33
New Jersey Plan, 112
New York, New York, 11, 20, 22, 33, 45, 52, 79, 82, 88, 93, 117-119
Newburgh, New York, 102
Newport, Rhode Island, 57
Nicholson, John, 124, 126, 129-131
Nonimportation, 19-20
North, Lord Frederick, 82
North American Land Company, 124-125
North River, 120
Nova Scotia, 11

Office of Finance, 76, 85-86, 88, 90, 92, 97, 104
Oxford, Maryland, 1, 3-4, 6-7

Paine, Thomas, 29, 54-55, 87, 134
Paris, France, 120
Parker and Company, Daniel, 105
Parliament, 16, 17, 22, 24, 30
Peace of Paris, 93, 100-101
Peale, Charles Willson, 55, 124
Penn, John, 15, 21-22, 24
Penn, Richard, 21-22, 108
Pennsylvania Packet, 27
Pensacola, Florida, 42
Peters, Richard, 80
Philadelphia, Pennsylvania, 4-6, 8-24, 26-34, 36-37, 39-40, 42-43, 45-47, 49, 52, 55, 57-58, 80-82, 88, 93, 98, 103, 110, 113, 115, 119, 123-124, 129-130
Pierce, William, 113
Polly, 23-24
Portsmouth, New Hampshire, 85
Potomac River, 6, 109, 122-124
Princeton, New Jersey, 38, 104
Privateering, 41-42
Prune Street jail, 130-132
Public debt, 97, 99, 117, 122

Quakers, 14, 27, 34, 37

Randolph, Edmund, 126
Reed, George, 112
Reed, Joseph, 56, 75, 78, 94-95, 99, 134
Reed, Thomas, 108
Residence Act, 123

Index 145

Revere, Paul, 24
Ridley, Katherine Livingston, 56-57
Ridley, Matthew, 84
Rittenhouse, David, 55
Robert Morris Inn, 7
Rochambeau, Jean Baptiste de Vimeur, Comte de, 57, 80-81
Rodney, Caesar, 31
Royal Charlotte, 17
Rutledge, John, 111

St. Augustine, Florida, 42
St. Christopher, 42
St. Eustatius, 36
St. George's Society for the Assistance of Englishmen in Distress, 26
Saratoga, New York, 47
Savannah, Georgia, 82, 93
Schuyler, Philip, 79
Schuylkill River, 15, 21, 46-47, 110, 112
Secret Committee, 27-28, 33, 35, 40-41, 48, 53-54, 115, 123
Senate, United States, 113-120, 122-124, 133
Severn, 11-12
Sherman, Roger, 29, 113-114, 133
Spain, 75, 79
Stamp Act, 17-19
State House, 8, 10, 15, 17-18, 20, 22-25, 27, 29-32, 43, 52, 55, 82, 103, 110-112
Steuben, Frederick William Augustus, Baron von, 79
Stiegel, Baron, 47
Superintendent of Finance. *See* Morris, Robert
Susquehanna River, 46, 122, 124

Taxation, 90-92, 101-102
Tea Act, 22-23
Tilghman Tench, 47, 53
Treaty of Paris, 13, 15
Trenton, New Jersey, 36, 75, 104, 112, 119

University of Leipzig, 84, 113
University of Pennsylvania, 56, 125

Valley Forge, Pennsylvania, 46, 49, 53, 112
Villiers, Coulon de, 9
Virginia Resolves, 111-112

Walnut Street prison, 53
Walton, George, 34
Ward, Artemas, 76
Wardens of the Port of Philadelphia, 19
Warren, James, 105
Washington, George, 9-10, 27-28, 34, 36-38, 42-43, 45-46, 48-49, 52-53, 57-58, 76-77, 79-84, 88, 91, 93-94, 99, 105-106, 108-114, 117-124, 126, 131, 133-134
Washington, Martha, 88, 119, 121
Wayne, Anthony, 79
West Indies, 6, 11-12, 40-42, 79, 117
West Point, New York, 58, 76
White, Esther Hewlings Newman, 44, 53
White, John, 13-14
White, Thomas, 21
White, William, 21, 44, 130
White Plains, New York, 52
Willing, Ann McCall, 15
Willing, Charles, 5, 7-9
Willing, Thomas, 5, 8-16, 19, 24-25, 28, 30, 47, 49, 53-54, 56-57, 88-89, 103, 130
Willing and Morris, 12-15, 28, 32-33, 40-41, 47, 54
Willing and Son, Charles, 5, 7-9, 11
Wilmington, Delaware, 46, 82
Wilson, James, 30, 55-57, 80, 88, 131
Wise, Captain, 19
Wise, Sarah, 4, 7

York, Pennsylvania, 46-47, 53
Yorktown, Virginia, 79-84, 88, 91

About the Author

FREDERICK WAGNER is Associate Professor of English at Hamilton College in Clinton, New York, where he has been teaching since 1969. Born in Philadelphia, raised in Moorestown and Haddonfield, New Jersey, he holds a Ph.D. degree from Duke University. For nearly a dozen years he was promotion manager for two major book publishers in New York City. He also has taught at the University of Oklahoma and at Duke. His only son, Alex, recently graduated with honors from Hamilton.

Writing about Mr. Wagner's *Famous Underwater Adventurers* in *The New York Times Book Review*, Henry W. Hubbard said, "He is certainly a good storyteller. His tales are vivid, humorous and informative. The more sophisticated reader will get special enjoyment from the author's gentle nuances and wry twists and learn a great deal, too." In a double-starred review of *Patriot's Choice*, Mr. Wagner's biography of John Hancock, *School Library Journal* commented, "A great deal of painstaking research has obviously gone into the preparation of this biography. . . . Invaluable for supplementary reading."

When *Submarine Fighter of the American Revolution* first was published, *Best Sellers* described it as "a fascinating story for readers of every age. In his work the author reaches the happy medium of easy style and scholarly research, producing a work which is at one time historically accurate and highly literary in quality." *The Horn Book* noted, "Boys will find fathers reading this intriguing research over their shoulders."